How to Create ANIMATION

By John Cawley and Jim Korkis
Foreword by John Musker

Books for the entertainment buyer

PIONEER

Designed and Edited by Hal Schuster
with the assistance of Bob Garsson

COVER CREDITS

Cover concept & design by Get Animated!
Buddy designed by Mitch Schauer
Buddy animation and model sheet by Kevin Wurzer
Buddy storyboard by Gary Conrad
Buddy cel color modeled and painted by Phyllis Craig
Buddy created under the direction of Pioneer Books, Inc. Buddy © 1990 Pioneer Books, Inc. All rights reserved

Library of Congress Cataloging-in-Publication Data
John Cawley and Jim Korkis
    How to Create Animation

    1.   How to Create Animation (animation)
I. Title

Published by Pioneer Books, Inc., 5715 N. Balsam Rd., Las Vegas, NV, 89130.

First Printing, 1990

Foreword

At the Chicago Film Festival of 1972, I heard Richard Williams speak at a retrospective of his work. Then, as now, his eyes had a bit of the madman about them as he spoke with awe and affection for this strange craft of animation.

Fast forward to 1974 and this time Chuck Jones was the "draw" at an animation festival at Northwestern University. There I heard, leavened by Jonesian quips and bon mots, tales of his obsession and dedication to the art form of character animation.

The words of these two men did much to inspire me to pursue this maddening craft. They both communicated to me the appealing notion that the more they learned about animation, the more they realized they didn't know.

Perhaps the words of the many exceptional talents interviewed for this book will similarly inspire some new students of animation. These professionals' love of the medium is clear, compelling, and maybe...catching.

John Musker,

September 19, 1990

John Musker is the co-writer, co-director and co-producer of the Academy Award winning Disney animated feature THE LITTLE MERMAID. Currently, he is handling the same duties, with his partner Ron Clements, on a new Disney feature, ALADDIN.

```
Prod. #282                              4-21-53
                                        Dir.: Tex Avery

                "DIXIELAND DROOPY"

Scene 1     Scene opens on a shot of the city dump.  A
            narrator speaks as the camera pans along.
            "LADIES AND GENTLEMEN.  THIS IS A TRUE STORY.
            THE STORY OF JOHN PETTIBONE, AN OBSCURE
            MUSICIAN WHOSE STRANGE LOVE FOR DIXIELAND MUSIC
            LIFTED HIM FROM THE DEPTHS OF THE CITY DUMP TO
            THE HEIGHTS OF THE HOLLYWOOD BOWL."  The camera
            stops at a little tumbled-down shack.

Scene 2     C. U. of the exterior of the little shack.  "THIS
            IS JOHN'S HOME - - -"

Scene 3     The voice continues as the camera pans slowly
            around the interior of the little shack.  "- - -
            NOTHING ELABORATE, RATHER PLAIN, BUT WITHIN
            THESE SIMPLE WALLS BEGAN THE FABULOUS CAREER OF
            A GREAT MUSICAL GENIUS, JOHN IRVING PETTIBONE."
            Droopy walks in and over to an old victrola.  He
            looks at the audience and says, "HELLO FOLKS".
            Droopy goes to an old trunk and puts on a straw
            hat, blazer and carries a record.  As he puts
            the record on the old victrola the narrator says,
            "HIS SINGLE AMBITION?  TO LEAD A DIXIELAND BAND
            IN THE HOLLYWOOD BOWL."  Droopy grabs a baton
            and begins to tap his foot.  He says, "ALL
            RIGHT BOYS, AH ONE, AH TWO".  Dixieland music
            begins.

Scene 4     "UNFORTUNATELY, HOWEVER, NOT ALL MUSIC LOVERS
            APPRECIATE DIXIELAND."  The night watchman of
            the city dump comes out of his office with his
            hands to his ears and stomps O. S.  Droopy is
            kicked out.  He looks back to see his record
            flying through the scene.  He just barely
            catches it and smilingly walks away.  The voice
            continues, "WELL JOHN, AT LEAST YOU STILL HAVE
            YOUR RECORD."

Scene 5     Out

Scene 6     Droopy walks off into perspective.

Scene 7     Droopy walks into a cafe with his record.

Scene 7A    Droopy walks over to the juke box.

Scene 8     Droopy disappears behind the juke box.  He opens
            the door at the back and enters the juke box.
            He puts his record on the player.
```

Top left: Script page from Tex Avery's DIXIELAND DROOPY, 1953 © *MGM*

Middle left: Storyboard sequence from DePatie-Freleng's Pink Panther TV series © *DePatie-Freleng*

Bottom left: Glen Keane's first scribble rough of Ratigan holding Fidget in THE GREAT MOUSE DETECTIVE © *Walt Disney Productions*

Right: Itchy model sheet from ALL DOGS GO TO HEAVEN; based on drawings by Don Bluth and John Pomeroy, cleaned up by John Pomeroy © *Goldcrest & Sullivan Bluth Ltd.*

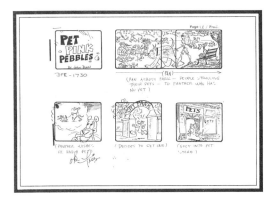

CONTENTS

Introduction

Animation has fascinated audiences for generations, but confusion and mystery continues to surround the process. To a degree, this is due to the way many of animation's pioneers delighted in making the work sound magical. It seemed like a wonderland where an artist could do anything because, as those pioneers often stated, "in animation there are no limitations."

The actual art of animation is not just an art; it also is a business. Except for student films and some independent artists, animation is not created by a single artist. Production of the average animated property takes an army of people, a factory full of mechanical equipment and a great deal of time, money and patience. In this book, readers will hear from people who are working every day as part of this massive system in an attempt to create the illusion of life.

This book is not another "how to draw" book filled with hundreds of illustrations for readers to trace and copy. Nor is it another "how we did it" book containing numerous anecdotes and stories from the golden age of animation. *How To Create Animation* tries to take a realistic and practical look at the process of creating animation today.

What makes this book unique is the series of interviews with the artists, directors and producers responsible for many of the animated properties now appearing in theaters, on television and home video. They discuss how they got into the business, their opinions on their particular job and their day-to-day routine. Their recommendations to aspiring artists should prove helpful and enlightening to anyone interested in animation.

We have included some chapters to help define terms and provide even a novice with a basic foundation of knowledge about animation. To help put the subject in proper perspective, we also have included interviews with some of animation's legendary creators—those whose work has inspired today's artists.

Readers of this book will gain a better understanding of the great amount of effort and thought behind even the simplest cartoon. They will learn a good deal about the business of animation and the people in it. This book is designed to be a valuable and necessary guide to how animation is created today.

Acknowledgements: In addition to those who were kind enough to let us interview them and several private collectors who allowed us to borrow illustrative material, we should additionally thank Joe Adamson, Jeff LaFlamme, Pam Martin, and Harry McCracken.

***

All interviews are by John Cawley unless otherwise noted as being by Jim Korkis.

Recognizing Animation

The most recognized form of animation—the one covered in detail in this book—often is called cel animation. This is what the layman thinks of when referring to "cartoons." This method begins with someone drawing an image. (For this reason, it occasionally is referred to as "hand drawn" animation.) This image is transferred to a cel (originally made of celluloid, these transparent sheets are now made of acetate). When the cel is placed over a background and photographed, it creates the illusion of a character in a setting.

However, animation is much more than "cartoons."

The term "animation" comes from the Latin word "anima," meaning "life," or "animare," meaning "to breathe life into." "Animation" describes a wide range of techniques that create an illusion of motion by shooting a frame at a time.

Animation is accomplished by a concept called "persistence of vision." When a single picture is flashed at the eye, the brain retains that image longer than it actually is registered on the retina. When a movie projector flashes a series of pictures in rapid order (particularly with the images only slightly changed), the effect is one of continuous motion. The brain remembers the previous picture when it is seeing the next picture. Persistence of vision is what makes all movies work. Today, films are projected at a standard 24 frames (images) per second.

Animation is more than merely recording in real time what the camera sees. In animation, each frame is shot separately. Anything can be made to move using the motion picture camera frame by frame: drawings, puppets, rocks, even stationary people in a process called "pixilation." The cost for such creative freedom is expensive. It can take several days to photograph or shoot a mere minute of screen time, not taking into account the work done previously to allow the filming to take place, such as drawing or sculpting.)

So while the U.S. may consider animation to be "cartoons," TV shows, feature films and an occasional commercial, the art form has a much broader scope. As stated above, any inanimate (or even animate) object can become animated when photographed frame by frame. If you were to travel the world, you would find a wide range of animated films. Many of these are short subjects, similar in length, though not in content, to the theatrical shorts by Disney, Fleischer, MGM, and Warner in the Twenties, Thirties, Forties and Fifties. These shorts might run on local TV or at international film festivals.

Then there is the animation that happens all around with little notice. The many who were dazzled by the mixture of live action and animation in *Who Framed*

Roger Rabbit, might be surprised at how much live action and animation they've already seen. Since films have begun, animation has been a constant part of the world of special effects. Dinosaurs, giant apes, space creatures, robots, mythological creatures and almost everything imaginable have come to life in live action films through animation.

For those who may wish to explore beyond the world of cel animation, we offer this brief listing of some of the other more enduring forms of animation.

Clay Animation

Instead of using drawings, some animators use clay mixtures and synthetic substitutes like Plasticine to create a three dimensional image. (Real clay can dry out under hot studio lights, resulting in things falling apart.) The earliest clay films in the U.S. were those by Helen Dayton in 1916. Even Max Fleischer, best known for his Popeye and Betty Boop cartoons, experimented with clay in a 1921 Koko the Clown film. It wasn't until the late Fifties that a clay animation project received popular attention. Art Clokey devised a children's TV series that featured the adventures of a little green boy named Gumby and his orange pony, Pokey.

Currently the "king of clay animation" is Will Vinton. Vinton's trademarked "Claymation" process brought life to the California Raisins as a series of commercials and then in their own TV specials. (Cel animation was used for a Saturday morning version of the Raisins.) Thanks to the success of Vinton's work, clay animation is being used more extensively from commercials t*Pee Wee's Playhouse*.

One of the more successful of these "new" animators is Jimmy Picker of Pickermation, who was responsible for *Sundae In New York* (1983), where Mayor Ed Koch sings *New York, New York* as he travels through the city.

Computer Animation

Computer technology is transforming the world of animation every day. It quickly is becoming one of the most visible forms of the art due to its heavy use in commercials for rotating logos and other graphics.

There are many misunderstandings about this newest form of animation. In the first place, the computer does not draw (yet). It still needs a human programmer or artist to input information through a variety of methods. The computer saves time and money because it can rotate the object, rotate the point of view and, if given the proper information, it can have the object move or float.

Computer animation began in the Sixties with films like James Whitney's *Catalogue* (1961), which made use of an analog computer. Since that time, computer animation has moved forward from just manipulating simple lines and shapes, to creating complex three-dimensional logos. It became a tool for movie special effects' teams in such films as *Tron* (1982).

The area of character animation has been stretched through such films as *The Adventures of Andre and Wally B.* and the Academy Award winning *Tin Toy*, both done by Pixar (an offshoot of Lucasfilm). There are now a number of programs that home computer users can purchase to create their own animation.

Computer animation also is being used to assist cel animation. One area being worked on is the use of computers to do the inbetweening of an animator's key drawings. Another is in the creation of backgrounds for cel animated productions. For example, a computer manipulated the mechanical clockwork interiors for Disney's *The Great Mouse Detective*. They can even color the films, replacing the cel process entirely.

Perhaps the most popular usage of computer animation (or graphics as it is sometimes called) is in video games. Simple dots of light bouncing across a screen have been replaced by three-dimensional figures doing battles with all creatures imaginable.

Other Hands

Not all animation drawn by hand becomes cel animation. Such avant garde animators as Norman McLaren drew directly on the 35mm film. Other independent animators still may use animation paper, but draw the finished art directly on the sheet with such medium as chalk, ink, markers or just pencil.

Puppet Animation

Though not common in the U.S., puppet animation is recognized and encouraged in Europe and the East. In puppet animation, most puppets have an armature of wood, metal or wire. This armature is a skeleton that allows the puppet to move slightly at body joints like elbows and knees and maintain that position while it is being photographed. To achieve different expressions, the animator will often change the heads on the puppets.

Most of the leading puppet animators have come from overseas. One of the better known, George Pal, achieved great acclaim in the U.S, as a result of his work on his Puppetoon shorts of the Thirties and Forties. Pal's knowledge of animation and special effects later came into play when he was a feature film producer, creating such classics as *The Time Machine* and *War of the Worlds*.

Usually puppets are comical or caricatured figures. Most readers have probably seen some of the Rankin/Bass puppet animated TV specials like the holiday classic, *Rudolph the Red Nosed Reindeer*, with a caricature of Burl Ives as a snowman. The more realistic armatures and figures would usually fall in the category of stop motion animation.

Puppet animation does not include projects like the Muppets, which are manipulated in real time as actual puppets. Neither would Gerry Anderson's Supermarionation be considered animation. His shows, such as *Thunderbirds, Supercar* and *Fireball XL-5*, featured marionettes (puppets) suspended by control wires.

Silhouette or Shadow Animation

Silhouette animation, once a somewhat popular alternative to cel animation, is one of the more uncommon forms of animation today. This process uses paper cutouts placed between the camera and a light source, allowing the viewer to see only the shadows.

One of the most famous animators to use this technique was the German-born Lotte Reiniger, who in 1926 completed the animated feature, *The Adventures of*

Prince Achmed. Reiniger continued to produce animated films (including a sound and color remake of *Achmed*) up to her death in the 1980s.

Stop Motion Animation

One of the most frequently viewed forms of animation in the U.S. (outside of cel animation), stop motion animation might be considered an offshoot of puppet animation. The concept is similar, in that a model figure is moved frame by frame to create the illusion of life. These models of such realistic figures as dinosaurs and aliens often have found their way into films as special effects.

Will Vinton's CALIFORNIA RAISINS

The undisputed father of stop motion is Willis O'Brien, responsible for many films that inspired generations of audiences, including the original *The Lost World* (1924) and *King Kong* (1933). One of O'Brien's assistants was Ray Harryhausen, who went on to even greater fame with his science fiction films such as *Earth vs. the Flying Saucers* (1956), *20 Million Years to Earth* (1957) and a series of films based on the stories of Sinbad the Sailor. In an attempt to separate from "animation," Harryhausen named his process "Dynamation" (and later "Dynarama" when doing wide screen films).

Steps in the Making of Animation

Animation can be traced back to ancient civilizations, where early artists tried various methods to capture the illusion of movement. With the introduction of movie film, a standardized process developed so that cartoon animation could be produced successfully.

The animation process is complex, time-consuming and labor intensive—factors that can make it look unattractive to many producers and studios. While a live action film or TV show can be filmed in a matter of days or weeks, a similar animated project might take many months or even years to complete.

The steps in animation have changed greatly over the years. As some studios modernized with computers, others preferred to maintain the more classic steps. The need to increase production and lower costs have caused some studios to send work overseas for completion. Some studios now handle several different types of productions and follow different steps for each.

The following chronological breakdown of steps in the making of an animated cartoon is based on the standard procedure used for decades. Some of these steps take place concurrently with other steps. Though the steps have been modified or changed over the years, most studios still explain animation procedure in the traditional fashion presented here. We've tried to update the process via notes whenever appropriate.

STORY.

Every project begins with a story. Sometimes the producer might generate the idea and assign it to a writer. Other times, it may originate with the writer. The writer often writes a complete script, similar in form to a live action script.

In TV production, the writer is one of the more powerful forces. The script must be approved by the network prior to the beginning of production. This causes studios to avoid altering the script, since any alteration also must be approved by the network. (Since waiting for approvals, as well as making any network-requested changes, can cause delays, few changes will be made within the studio.)

STORYBOARD.

The script is translated into a storyboard, which resembles a huge comic strip. A series of one-panel pencil sketches, showing the action, are pinned up in sequence on a huge board. Underneath each sketch may be dialog or action descriptions. Once completed, the board can be discussed and altered simply by re-arranging the panels. These panels can range from simple stick figures to elaborate full-color sketches.

For TV, storyboards are done on standardized form paper. Most of these forms allow space not only for dialog or action description, but also for translation. The TV storyboard artist also wields a lot of power. Since his board is sent overseas (where the animation is done), it becomes a firm blueprint for many elements from character staging to scenic design to action. Like the script, the storyboard (or simply "board") is sent to network for approval.

RECORDING THE VOICES.

After the story has been approved, actors are hired to record the voices of the cartoon characters. The vocal performances given by these actors may influence bits of business or how the animator will visualize the character. Often voice actors will provide the voice for more than one character in a project. (In some foreign countries, such as Japan, the voices are actually recorded after animation is completed.)

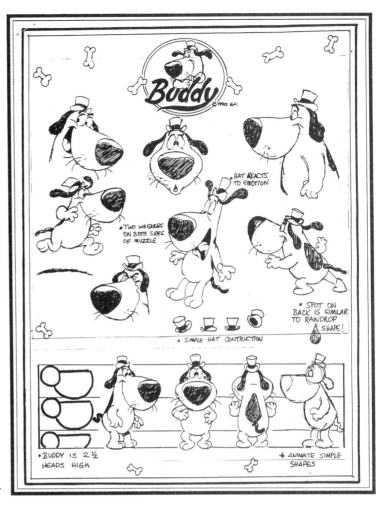

TRACK READER.

This technician listens to the dialog and literally measures each vowel and consonant of every word. These words are written onto exposure sheets (often called "X-sheets"), where each space corresponds to a frame of film. This is a visual record of dialog so that action can be synchronized with the sound. Overseas productions, such as TV series, use the track reader slightly differently as discussed in the Directing section below.

MODELS.

Final models are drawn of the characters. Model sheets are created so that each character will always be drawn the same and stay "on model." The sheets can be as elaborate as giving details on how to draw the character or merely showing the character in various poses. Through the Seventies, these sheets were made into stats and distributed to the artists. More recently, these sheets are simply photocopied. Sometimes three-dimensional statues will be made so an animator may view the character from all sides and in different lighting.

A model sheet assists all the artists in maintaining a consistent look. Some may be merely a collection of animation drawings from a key animator, while others, like this one for Buddy, may include drawing and animation guides. Model sheet prepared by Kevin Wurzer.
Note Buddy keys, storyboards and final clean-up on front cover of this book.
© Pioneer Books, Inc.

LAYOUT.

Using the storyboard as a guide, the layout crew designs the sets for the film. With the help of the director, they determine the staging of the production by designing linear drawings as guidelines for the animators. In some productions, the layout artist also draws the character for proper posing. The layouts also are used by artists who paint the backgrounds—paintings over which cels will be placed for photographing. Layout and background both help to establish the mood for a film.

For TV productions sent overseas, there is frequently only a series of "key layouts" prepared. These are a small number of layouts selected from major scenes for establishing shots. Actual production layouts, used by animators and background artists, will be done by the layout staff overseas.

DIRECTING.

The animation director is the one person involved with all phases of the process. With the storyboard approved, voices recorded and models created, it is his responsibility to time the picture. That is to say, he determines how long or short scenes will run and which animators will be handling which scenes. Since each animator has a different temperament, acting ability or artistic talent, the director must attempt to assign scenes and characters according to an animator's strengths. Some may excel at more realistic human characters while others may be more talented at creating certain types of movement. The director directs the animators in terms of what the character must accomplish emotionally or physically in a scene, along with the overall tempo of the scene so it will match the rest of the film.

For overseas production, the directors are often called "sheet directors." Since these directors will not work in close proximity with the overseas animators, they put all their direction on the exposure sheets.

They start by timing out the storyboard, adding footage (time) between lines of dialog for action to take place. This is called "slugging" as the director is literally calling for a "slug" of film to be placed in the track to separate the lines of dialog. This "slugged board" is given to a track editor and reader, who will add the necessary silent parts to the sheets.

The sheet director then receives the entire show (or segment) timed on the sheets and goes through them, making notes for the animator. These could be directions as to when to start and stop certain actions, number of frames needed for taking steps, etc. Some directors will draw elaborate posing on the sheets to direct the animator.

These sheets are the key to overseas production and the foreign staff will use the storyboard and exposure sheets to create the entire show. Some directors have referred to this process as "directing by remote control." It is usually the last step taken (until the animation is ready for editing) by the U.S. staff using a foreign crew.

ANIMATION.

Following the storyboard and the director's exposure sheets as well as personal direction, the animator brings the characters to life. Using the model sheets, the animator sketches out what he thinks the character is feeling and how the character should be doing a certain action. He makes "extreme" drawings for these actions.

Depending upon the scene, he may make only a few key pose drawings or many drawings to clearly indicate the character's movement. The more routine detailed work will be accomplished by other artists. For example, in a scene of a man running, an animator might provide only the drawing of the foot leaving the floor, another drawing of the foot in the air and a final drawing of the foot touching the floor again.

In limited animation, the animator learns to work with separate elements of a character. To make a character blink, for example, the artist will draw the eyes on a separate sheet of paper from that of the head. This way it is necessary only to draw the blinking eyes—not the entire face.

ASSISTANT ANIMATORS AND INBETWEENERS.

The assistant animator improves on the rough sketches of the animator, cleaning up the lines,and adding details or incidental action to the extreme drawings. Next the inbetweeners fill in the simplest drawings that come between the drawings already completed. These tasks are often performed by the same individual, simply referred to as an assistant.

CLEAN-UP.

After a scene has been completely animated, it goes to clean-up, where artists literally clean up the drawings. They make sure all characters remain on model. It is one of the less creative steps in the animation process, but oddly enough, one of the most important. Good clean-up can improve a poorly drawn scene, but bad clean-up can destroy the best animation. A good clean-up artist is one who can enhance drawings without changing their impact. (Some clean-up people will actually re-animate as they clean-up, altering original staging, posing and intentions!) Due to this situation, studios more and more are looking for good, professional clean-up talent.

ANIMATION CHECKING.

At this point, a scene is checked to make certain everything is ready for the final processes. The scene is checked to see that all drawings called for on the exposure sheet are in the scene. They also ensure that the mechanics, such as the figure lining up properly with the background, are right.

PENCIL TEST.

At some studios, a test reel of the pencil sketches is filmed and then screened so it can be checked for staging, smoothness of action and proper expression among other things. Today, most studios use video systems to test the rough animation. These systems have become so sophisticated with computers that some require the artist (or cameraman) to shoot the scene only once. They can then program the computer to "expose" (or screen) the drawings in any order or timing the operator wishes. This process continues until the desired effect is reached and the computer then prints out the sequence order selected.

BACKGROUND ARTISTS.

While all this is going on, background artists have produced color background paintings from the pencil layout drawings. The landscapes, scenery, buildings, interiors, etc. need to be ready once the approved animation goes to inking. As studios move more into computerization, this is another step that is being taken over. For example, the Disney studio hopes to move to computer backgrounds by the middle of the Nineties. The layout will be scanned by the computer and the background artists will assign color from a pre-determined template.

Again, for overseas production, the U.S. studio will generally produce only a number of background "keys." These will be small (often around 4"x6") paintings of some of the key layouts. The overseas studio will use them to base their painting on.

INKING.

In the old days, artists would trace over, by hand, the animator's pencil sketches onto a piece of transparent acetate called a cel. The ink lines were in colors corresponding to the paints that would be used on the cels. This kept the lines smooth and unobtrusive.

In the Fifties, Disney began using a Xerographic process, similar to that of photocopying, that allowed the drawing to be transferred to a cel. This greatly speeded up the process of animation and eliminated a major expense (and sadly, many jobs). Another significant effect this had on animation was the look it gave the art form. Inkers always did smooth, thick color lines. The new process, since it was an exact copy of the drawing, looked more illustrative. This was due to the scratchy black lines now surrounding the paints. Since then, more colors have been added and they can make the photocopied line a variety of colors (gray, brown, etc.).

Hand inking is still done on occasion for effects or when multiple colors or light colors are needed. For example, a character with blonde hair might have that hair inked with a yellow line.

PAINTING.

A staff of painters applies the specific colors on the reverse side of the cel. The coloring throughout the picture is kept uniform by a "color key" person. This person works with the director and other departments to create color models of the characters. These color combinations must be suitable not only for the character, but must go with the many varied painted backgrounds.

In many productions, there will have to be models of the same character showing the colors in daylight, at night, in shadows, etc. They also must make allowances for the depth of the cel. A color will look quite different when it is alone on top of a background and when it is underneath a cel with a different character. (Even though cels are clear, they do have density, which alters the color value.)

Due to the steep expense of painting, studios doing all their work in the U.S. are seeking alternate methods to reduce costs. One solution is to send only the painting overseas to foreign countries. Another is to send the painting to locations in the U.S. where wages are lower than in primary animation areas such as Los Angeles or New York.

Finally, some studios are beginning to color their projects by computer. The computer scans the animation drawing and an operator uses a wand to indicate an area of the drawing (say a hand) on the computer screen and select a color. The computer instantly fills the area with that color and the color images can be put onto a previously scanned background, creating a color scene. Some TV shows have used this process for several years. In 1990, Disney released *The Rescuers Down Under*, the first theatrical feature colored by computer. Though this system does save considerable time and money, the equipment is expensive. It also eliminates the cel, which has become a popular collectible.

PAINT CHECKING.

Assembly and double-checking of all inked and painted material along with background in preparation for the camera department.

CAMERA.

Cels are packaged and sent with the background to the animation camera. If the background does not change throughout a scene, it is the base for all cels in that scene. The cameraman photographs the animation and backgrounds by following the camera instructions on the exposure sheets. A single frame of film is exposed at a time. A scene of only a few seconds on the screen may take hours to photograph. The film is then sent to the lab and a print is made.

EDITING.

The cutting department takes the prints and cuts them into a reel, synchronizing the dialog with the picture. This is called a work print. From this work print, sound effects and appropriate music are added. An orchestra may be involved in recording the score. It usually is necessary to put all of these on more than one track and the tracks are prepared for an assembling process called dubbing.

For productions animated overseas, this also is the step where retakes are called. The footage that has arrived from the foreign studio will be checked for mistakes ranging from camera (a cel may have been left out for one shot, causing a "pop"), to animation (it may be poorly drawn), to color (a wrong color of paint). The retakes are requested, and depending on the schedule, will be cut into the final work print later. Sometimes schedules are so tight for Saturday morning shows that there is no time for retakes, causing mistakes to go on the air.

DUBBING.

Dialog, music and sound effects are re-recorded from as many as 11 separate tracks onto one balanced track. For most productions, a minimum of two tracks are maintained. One contains only the dialog; the other has music and effects. This is to facilitate translating the dialog for foreign editions.

LABORATORY.

The negative is cut to match the work print and the final track is then combined with the picture and printed to achieve the finished product. [or]

VIDEO POST PRODUCTION.

For TV, the correct negative and tracks are taken to a video post production house. There the negative and track are put onto videotape for broadcast on TV. At this time, various aspects from video effects and titles as well as color correction will take place.

How to Write for Animation

A BRIEF HISTORY

"We never used writers," is a common statement from many people who worked in the Golden Age of animation. It is one of many misconceptions about animation. Though it is true most of the classic shorts and features never had what might be considered a formal script, writers were a key part of the animation process. They were called "storymen," a term resented by some.

Depending on the studio, these individuals could develop plots and characters, tie gags together, create storylines, or write dialog and narration. In some respects, they were the "unsung" heroes of the Golden Age of animation. After all, many people believe what made Mickey Mouse a hit was that he talked. Certainly what helped make many of the Warner characters so popular was as much what they said as what they did. Like too many of the talents in that era, the writer's work often went uncredited on the screen.

At Warner, there were, among others, Michael Maltese (who wrote many of the great parodies starring Daffy Duck and Porky), Warren Foster, Ben Hardaway, Tedd Pierce, Lloyd Turner, Dave Monahan and Rich Hogan (who wrote three of the first four Bugs Bunny cartoons). Disney had such greats as Bill Peet, Carl Barks, Ralph Wright, Homer Brightman, Dick Huemer, Ted Sears, Dick Kinney, Joe Grant. Other studios had storymen like Heck Allen, Bill Scott, Jack Mercer, Tom Morrison and John Dunn. Without the work of men like these, the history of animation would be a much different and poorer story.

To see the effect these men had on their studios, one need only look at the output of Warner and Hanna-Barbera in the early Sixties. As Hanna-Barbera began building an empire with the original Huckleberry Hound, Yogi Bear and the Flintstones, several of the key Warner writers, including Maltese and Foster, were hired. As Warner cartoons became flatter, the H-B series thrived and the characters became new cartoon superstars. Some tried to blame the weak humor of the new Warner shorts on lower budgets, but most Warner shorts had five times the budget of a H-B cartoon. The key difference was the writing. One of the weakest animated television cartoon series was *Rocky and Bullwinkle*. It became a major success through the writing skills of storymen like Alan Burns and Chris Hayward (who later developed live action shows like *The Mary Tyler Moore Show*) and Bill Scott.

THE WRITER TODAY

As animation continues to grow, so has the importance of the writer. In the world of TV, writers are carefully sought out to prepare the scripts (which must be approved by networks before any artwork even begins). All studios and networks complain of a shortage of good writers. This complaint is hard to correct, though, since networks and studios shy away from new talent. They prefer to rely on standard writers who have a track record of meeting deadlines (a major factor in TV animation) and keeping material within proper standards (extremely important to networks sensitive to public interest and parent groups). This desire to maintain a consistent production schedule keeps a large number of just average storytellers in business.

Feature films also are beginning to feel the need for stronger stories. In decades past, various development artists, animators and directors would create memorable scenes based on a general storyline. The end result would be just that: memorable scenes, but little story. It wasn't until critics and audiences began taking note that some films were better written than others that studios began to make a connection. Films with strong stories and (sometimes) lesser animation could do better critically and at the box office than a feature with excellent animation but a sagging story. This trend has caused the Disney studio to insist on a script being completed before any major production work is done on a feature.

Another industry misconception is that only animators can write for animation. If such a connection were true, then the only people who could write plays, films or TV shows would be actors. Good writing is simply that: good writing. Writers working in animation need special insight, due to the nature of the industry, but do not need to have any actual animation training.

GETTING STARTED

Animation scripts for TV or films look similar to scripts for live action. Most of the rules in story, plot and character development apply equally to both. The only major differences are the descriptions and staging.

When dealing with animation, the writer must remember that everything is created from scratch. There are no ready-built sets, no pool of character actors, etc. All details must be in the script. For this reason, animation scripts tend to be heavier on detail. Though the script will at one point be converted to art in storyboards and layouts, the writer must fill in enough details for the initial art to begin.

In staging, the key to remember is that in animation, the camera doesn't move. The writer will still use terms like "pan" (to indicate the camera "moving" left or right, up or down) and "pull back" (to have the camera "move" farther away), but they must keep in mind that the camera can't actually do that. The art creates the illusion that such movement is taking place. In a pan, for example, the camera doesn't move, the background does!

Another popular expression is that there are no limits to animation. Animation actually has two very hard and fast limits: time and money. The more elaborate a scene, the more of both it will take. In today's industry that just isn't available. Where Disney might have taken decades to bring a film to completion, current schedules demand film turnaround (from script to screen) to be around two years!

This is not to say that the art form has become more limited. What it means is that those producing (and writing) the films need to plan more fully. If you plan a massive spectacle with scenes of hundreds of characters mingling through a courtyard, it had better be balanced with scenes of utter simplicity. A surprise to many writers is that these simple scenes can be the most effective.

THE SCRIPT FORM

As said earlier, the script form for animation is identical to that for live action films. About the only major difference is that in animation, the writer will not number the scenes. Though the sample shown is a common script form, there is no "universal" script format. One that follows the general rules will do fine.

THE TV PROCESS

Writing for TV is the most common form of animation writing. This is due to the large amount of production occurring. With (now) four networks handling Saturday morning programming and many new majors getting into the syndication market, the animation industry is truly booming.

When selling to TV, one must remember that the writer must please many individuals, ranging from producers to story editors to studio executives and network personnel. Getting a script through the TV system takes several steps, all of which can be painful. Of considerable importance is remembering who TV animation is aimed at: children. Don't attempt to break in with an earth-shattering tale. As discussed earlier, most of the networks and TV producers like "*safe.*" During a recent writing class for a studio, the teacher's advice was: if a writer even wonders if something (an act, a word, an idea) will be questionable, *don't use it!*

Generally the first step is the "springboard" or "log line." These are one to two-sentence storylines. (The term "log line" is sometimes used because these resemble the type of listing one would see in a TV log or guide.) This should be an entertaining way to describe the plot. Remember, you're writing this so that someone reading it will want to see the show. Springboards are almost always done on "spec" (speculation)—that is to say, no cost to the studio.

A successful springboard will be developed into a "premise." (Some studios bypass springboards and start with the premise.) This is usually a one to two-page synopsis of the story. Length of the premise usually is based on the length of the segment. Popular segment lengths are five to six minutes, around 11 minutes or 23 minutes (a half hour show). Again, this element must sell the story. It should be fast reading and highlight key scenes (humorous things in a comedy; action scenes in an action show). Some studios will pay you to write a premise, others won't.

The next step will be an "outline." This is approximately half the page count of a script. (The popular rule of thumb dictates that two pages of script equal one minute of screen time.) An outline for a half hour (22-minute) script would be around 20 pages. The outline is perhaps best described as a storybook telling of the script. The writer will use descriptions and actual (proposed) lines of dialogue. Most studios will pay for an outline.

If, after all of these processes, the story is still a "go," the writer will take it to script form. At this time, the writer will finally put the story into an actual script. It's here that you will break down the descriptions, dialogue and camera "moves." All studios, of course, pay you to write the script.

Most studios allow approximately three weeks for this process. The first week is on log lines and premises. Week two is to create an outline. The third week is writing the script. At the busiest time of production, this time frame can be squeezed to just over a week. Another common practice at studios is to expect at least one script re-write for the fee paid you.

THE FEATURE PROCESS

Writing for features is not too different from writing for TV. You still must generally prepare some form of springboard or premise to submit your idea. Even though you may be dealing with one studio, your project/script will have to go through many hands before it finally is picked up.

SUBMITTING MATERIAL

This can be a little tricky. Unless you have discussed the material in advance and the studio has asked to see your writings you may get no response except the return of your envelope, unopened. Most studios today will not look at unsolicited writing, for fear of later legal action. Even though you believe your idea is totally original, it is quite common for studios to have similar projects in development. The Disney studio generally has more than a dozen titles in development in any month and these titles change frequently. Even a small studio may have dozens of shows in development or script stages.

Don't think because a show is on the air, a studio will gladly look at a script for the series. Once again, recent legal cases have made studios wary. Many will not look at even a sample script if it contains their characters. When in doubt, send some work samples based on characters not in production at the studio to which you are submitting material.

As previously mentioned, TV will offer you the best chance for breaking into the business. The best thing to do is to call the studio in advance and ask to whom you could submit materials. Usually, they will request a sample script from you. Once again, be certain it does not feature their characters. Due to the large number of submissions, it can sometimes take months for the studio to get back to you. Most will, so be patient.

Features are very hard to break into. Most of the studios producing features have their own development departments. For your idea to get in, as one head of development put it, "it would have to be nothing less than the world's greatest idea." Once again, most of those who are looking will want to see a sample (feature) script. Oddly, both feature productions and TV productions often prefer to see a live action script sample. They feel it is easier to teach a good writer to write more visually than to teach a visual person to be a good writer.

RECOMMENDED READING FOR WRITERS

To assist in strengthening your writing style, you might want to check out the following books:

The Elements of Style, William Strunk, Jr./E.B. White, McMillan Publishing Company.

Teleplay: An Introduction to Television Writing, Coles Trapnell, Hawthorn Books, Inc.

Screenplay: the Foundations of Screenwriting, Syd Field, Delta Books.

A Look Back: Perspectives on Animation Production

Animation, as it is known today, is less than a century old.

Originally a novelty, like its fellow art form, motion pictures, animated films were simply short films of movement. Early audiences were less demanding and just the novelty of movement was sufficient to provide entertainment. Most early film efforts were not story oriented, but simple excuses for a series of slapstick gags or astounding visuals.

That's one of the reasons animators like Ub Iwerks and Otto Messmer could animate an entire cartoon themselves "straight through." That is to say, they could sit down and just start drawing and continue drawing until enough artwork existed for an animated cartoon. Iwerks once produced 700 drawings in a single day. "I've always had a competitive nature," Iwerks said during an interview. "I'd heard that Bill Nolan, who was doing Krazy Kat, had done five or six hundred drawings a day, so I really extended myself."

Those early animated cartoons (again, like their live action film counterparts) were more often than not regarded as product rather than art. Animators at Terrytoons have recounted the story of producer Paul Terry wandering through the studio with a ruler. When the stacks of drawings reached an arbitrary mark on the ruler, Terry declared the cartoon finished with work to begin on the next one. This is similar to live action films that were "finished" when the reel of film ended.

As the business of animation became more profitable, producers became more predatory. Though it was impossible to steal another cartoon studio's "star" (as live action studios often did), producers could steal the artists behind the stars. Max Fleischer's wife mentioned in an interview that Roy Disney used to come down to her husband's studio at lunch hour and steal away animators by offering them more money. Then Fleischer had to take five or six inbetweeners, get them in a room and say, "Look, you're gonna go home and look yourselves in the mirror and say, 'Tomorrow I'm gonna be an animator!'" Then the cycle would start all over again. This predatory nature is why many studios, such as Disney, preferred not to list the names of artists on their films.

As live action pictures developed into small stories, so did the animated shorts. Disney is credited with introducing the concept of storyboard, which allowed for more attention to story structure. However, as live action shorts grew into full-length feature films, animation remained short. Even though there are a handful of animated features from the Twenties and early Thirties, it took almost 20 years after the creation of feature motion pictures for Disney to release a major (and commercially successful) animated feature. Though others tried, Disney remained virtually alone for decades.

Most will agree it was Walt Disney and his studio that redefined the medium. He created a training program headed by Donald Graham that gave animators an opportunity to expand their artistic skills. While Messmer's Felix the Cat is usually cited as the beginning of character animation, it was Disney who expanded and refined the art of character animation. Yet even at Disney's, animators learned through the grueling experience of trial and error, establishing the traditions and guidelines often followed by today's animation studios.

Unlike today, the primary market for animation was the theatrical short cartoons shown before feature films in movie theaters. New cartoons appeared each week. They had to appeal to a broad audience composed of people of all ages, educational backgrounds and cultures. Since these were merely shorts, the studios generally didn't pay much attention to them. It was a time when animators could really please themselves over almost any other factor. Only if the short created a major character (that could be licensed to toys and comics) or won an Oscar did it receive any special attention. In fact, it wasn't until the massive growth of TV in the Fifties that most of these cartoons were ever re-shown after their initial release.

The men in the next four chapters all have had long and varied careers in the field of animation. They are respected pioneers who were responsible for animated cartoons that still entertain new generations of audiences. In the beginning, however, they were merely young men making decisions based on instinct, budget and immediate experience. Their philosophy and insights about the art were shaped by those early days of discovery. Each found things that worked and on the following pages, they share some of the secrets gained over the years.

Robert (Bob) Clampett was born in San Diego, Calif., May 8, 1913. When he was quite young, his family moved to Hollywood and for a while, they lived next door to Charlie Chaplin and his brother, Syd. While still in high school, he helped his aunt, Charlotte Clark, make the first Mickey Mouse dolls. After graduation from high school in 1931, he began as an animator for the Harman-Ising studio which was producing the Looney Tunes and Merrie Melodies series for Warner Brothers. When Leon Schlesinger took over the series, Clampett continued with the series and worked alongside many talented animation figures, including Tex Avery, Chuck Jones and Friz Freleng among others. During his 16 years with the studio, Clampett played a key role in the development of the Warner cartoons' style of humor and characters. As a director, his exaggerated style is instantly recognizable. Clampett continued to experiment and explore on his own, de-

Robert "Bob" Clampett

Q:

How did you get interested in animation?

A:

Actually, my interest in puppets and comic strips led to me going into animation. To me, puppets were cartoon figures that you could make come to life. I was intrigued with them and I would stage all sorts of shows with these puppets. It was considered a little odd back then for a boy to be interested in such things. Even when I was working at Warners, the guys really razzed me for "playing with dolls." With puppets, I wanted to create a fantasy world, peopled with characters so believable that an audience could lose themselves in the illusion. I always thought of puppets as "dimensional cartoons," one of the ways

my approach to puppetry differed from other puppeteers of the time.

Also, even as early as 12 years old, I was submitting cartoons to the Los Angeles Examiner and they were printing them. Many of the early animators, like Winsor McCay, came from working on newspaper strips. King Features saw my work and offered me a cartoonist's contract to start at $75 a week when I finished high school. But after I finished school, I joined up with Harman-Ising for $10 a week. That's how enchanted I was with the new medium of sound cartoons.

Q:

What was your first work in animation?

A:

Merrie Melodies started early

"BEANY"
© by
Bob Clampett

veloping projects involving such notables as Edgar Rice Burroughs and Charlie McCarthy. Clampett left Warner in 1946 to direct cartoons for Republic Pictures. They released only one short, It's A Grand Old Nag. Clampett then returned to one of his early skills and created a puppet show for TV, Time for Beany. It was an award-winning program and Clampett later used the characters and similar storylines for an animated series entitled Beany and Cecil. Before his death May 2, 1984, Clampett was a popular speaker at universities and conventions, where he spoke on the history of animation and showed film clips. At the time, his studio was supplying animation for commercials for a number of different clients. The following excerpts are from a series of interviews conducted with Clampett by Jim Korkis from 1978-1984.

in 1931 and I was given a number of secondary characters to animate in the very first one, *Lady Play Your Mandolin*. Even more than animation, I loved coming up with gags and story ideas. The first week, I came up with a sequence for the second Merrie Melodies done by Harman-Ising. Actually Hugh and Rudy encouraged me to come up with ideas, as did Leon Schlesinger when I went with him. I would get my animation pretty far along and then I would go in and kibitz with the story guys and pretty soon we'd get into talking about the story and I'd be throwing ideas with them. I always loved that.

Q:
Did working at the Warners Studio influence the animation?

A:
Definitely. Across the alley from us were sound stages and we'd see these great actors all day. Jimmy Cagney and Humphrey Bogart and other top Warner stars used to stick their heads in our windows to see how cartoons were made. We patterned a lot of things on them. Of course, we caricatured them many times, but I also feel that the brashness of their characters helped inspire some of our characters.

Q:
Were there any particular comedians who influenced your work?

A:
Of course. Bits and pieces, attitudes, actions, timing, poses, facial expressions, gags, etc. of the top comedians over the years

Model sheet of Beany for the animated BEANY & CECIL TV series

© Bob Clampett

have been very inspirational. I could get into many facets, but let me give you just one example. I got to know Harold Lloyd and I had long talks with him about how he constructed his silent comedies. I saw his *Freshman* football comedy many times and there was a gag in there that inspired a gag I used in *Bugs Bunny Gets the Boid*.

have Bugs land in the sand near the skeleton of a steer and when he comes to, he feels the ribs of the skeleton and thinks it is his own body. He cries and then to lighten the situation, I had Bugs make an aside to the audience, "Gruesome, isn't it?"

Pencil sketches drawn by Bob Clampett for the opening of early Looney Tunes' series

© Warner Bros.

When you're writing a story about Bugs out in the desert you say to yourself "what props do I have to work with?" Well, there's cactus, sand, the skull of a steer, bones and so forth. I remembered Lloyd's gag in which he was substituting for the tackling dummy in the sawdust pit. He is hit by a hard tackle and lands with one leg out of sight under the sawdust. Looking down, he sees a leg that has become disconnected from the tackling dummy and thinks it is his own leg. This was done very humorously.

That bit came to my mind just as I was thinking "what do you do with bones?" I got the idea to

Q:
How did you move up into direction?
A:

I had always wanted to move into direction because that way you had more control over the entire process. On my own, I was developing projects like a possible series on John Carter of Mars by Edgar Rice Burroughs, who wrote *Tarzan*. Anyway, Ub Iwerks, who had been brought in to do some Porky Pig cartoons, left and one Monday I walked in and was told "Ub's gone. You're the director now." That's how things happened in those days.

Q:

Why was the term "supervision" used instead of "director?"

A:

Leon Schlesinger called his directors "supervisors," which I believe he took from Irving Thalberg, who called his key film makers at MGM "supervisors." I think Leon was smart enough to know that if he called people "supervisor," the audience would think the supervisor was just the bookkeeper or the pencil lead dispenser. So, when Leon went to the race track, they'd say, "Hey, that was a great cartoon you drew last night, Leon." And he'd just smile. Remember, in those days people thought that Walt Disney did everything himself from drawing the animated cartoons to the comic strip to everything else. Sometimes even people in the business didn't know who was doing what. It has only been in recent years that some of these talented people have started to get credit for their work.

Q:

Why is some of your direction so wild?

A:

When I'm speaking at conventions, I get asked that question a lot. The only answer I can give is "That's just the way I saw the world." To me, it would have been odd to direct any other way. I remember when I was making *Porky in Wackyland,* which was very unusual for its time, Leon would walk into the projection room when I was running dailies and moan, "Oh no! Clampett's wet dream!" We only had about three weeks to make each short and a budget of about $3,000. I believe it was Ray Katz who used to say "We don't want quality, and we don't want it in the worst way." All that was important was that a cartoon was ready to meet the schedule for a play date at a theater. But some of us just had fun doing them. I guess that was our compensation for the time pressure.

Q:

How did Warners develop so many memorable characters?

A:

I think what I enjoy talking about most are the things that lead to things. In other words, in the creation of an animated character, people are too ready to say "How was Mickey Mouse created? Oh, a mouse was on the drawing board and somebody said, 'Of course! Mickey Mouse!'" We all know it doesn't happen that way. Anything that is good is an evolution of thought over a period of time. Everyone contributes something. Very few characters ever appeared fully born. For me, some of my characters and gags were influenced by films.

Q:

What was an especially influential film for you?

A:

When I saw *The Lost World* (1924), it was one of the most exiting things I ever saw in my life. It was one of the first films that used stop motion animated figures and I think in many cases the fluidity of Willis O'Brien's animation in the film was even superior to what he later did on *King Kong* (1933). O'Brien got a certain sympathetic personality into these characters. I used my own version of this same basic story plot right from the beginning on my *Time for Beany*

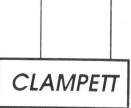

CLAMPETT

Bob Clampett pencil sketch of Tweety

Warner Bros.

To JIM

WOTS OF WOVE and WUCK!

from Tweety

and SODY and BOB CLAMPETT
JUNE 19, 1982

puppet show. Captain Huffenpuff was really my version of the Professor Challenger figure and Cecil, the Sea Sick Sea Serpent, owes a lot to O'Brien's dinosaur.

Q:
How did you envision the characters on Beany and Cecil?
A:

My key characters have so many facets to their personality, and are such well rounded characters, that oversimplification doesn't really give the complete true picture of each character. As I am thinking up what my characters do or say, I instinctively know what is in character for them and what's not. That's true for all really good characters.

Basically, Beany is the "identification figure" through whose eyes you see the world. You see all these wonderful sights and adventures through a child's eyes. I wanted him to have a little bit of Charlie McCarthy's precociousness, so that he wasn't a "goody-goody."

Cecil is all heart. He doesn't know his own power. He's lonely. He was raised as the world's only sea serpent. He was a different color. He felt different than everyone else. Yet, he is always looking for the good in everybody. He's very trusting and he believes in people. The thing that people love about Cecil is when he does finally catch on that he's been taken, usually by Dishonest John, he goes into action and he can do fabulous things.

Speaking of Dishonest John, he is a happy villain. Some guys will try to sell you a car but they give you all this schmaltz while trying to pick your pockets. If you catch them, they admit they were crooked but you still like them. Basically, Dishonest John

is like that.

Q:
Should all characters have that depth of background?
A:

I think the fact that the characters were so real to me was the reason they worked so well, not only on the puppet show but in animation and all the other mediums like comic books. The audience accepted the illusion we attempted to convey because the background of the characters was so rich that people believed in them. I've been told that little babies would go up to the TV screen and kiss it when Beany was on. In other words, he was very real to them, just as he was to me.

Q:
Any closing thoughts?
A:

I've never put this into words before, but I think animation is a marvelous medium. An artist can take a pencil and put the city of Rome or a strange planet on a small piece of paper and have a character do anything at all that comes to his imagination. There is no other medium that allows you to so control every frame of film to exactly what you want to have happen. It's a wonderful medium.

I've seen animators come from various backgrounds and with various talents. Some are excellent artists, or good cartoonists, and some aren't even that good to begin with. But, if those just getting started in animation love it and work at it the way we did, study and get pointers from the people that have been in it for awhile, I think they can do fabulous things.

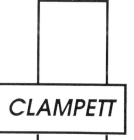

CLAMPETT

John Fredrick (Jack) Hannah was born in Nogales, Ariz., Jan. 5, 1913. He joined the Disney studios in 1933 and spent five years as an animator, another five years in the story department and close to 20 years as a director. During his career at Disney, he directed eight shorts which were nominated for Academy Awards. He worked on more than 100 cartoons featuring Donald Duck, Chip 'n' Dale, Humphrey the Bear and other characters. He also directed 14 hour-long TV shows for the Disneyland TV series, including many skits with Walt Disney at his desk talking with Donald Duck. He left the studio in 1959 and worked briefly at the Walter Lantz studio. There, in addition to directing shorts, he was responsible for directing live action/ animation seg

John F. "Jack" Hannah

Q:

How did you first join Disney?

A:

I was seeking work in the commercial art field during the Depression and I grabbed on to any job that came along since I needed the money to live. I went to an art agency with my portfolio and they suggested I try Disney. I protested that I wasn't a cartoonist but a commercial artist but the guy kept insisting. So, I took my portfolio over to Disney and was given a two-week tryout. I started there Jan. 31, 1933 as an inbetweener making about $16 a week. Gradually I moved up from inbetweener to second assistant and then finally a first assistant.

Q:*What was it like being an assistant?*

A:

I assisted different top animators like Ham Luske, Dick Huemer, Les Clark, Dick Lundy and several others. My greatest learning experience was being assigned as an assistant to Norm Ferguson. He animated very loosely. I progressed faster because I had to follow up the toughest guy. He was very loose and had a terrific sense of flow. When you picked up his roughs, you had to start from scratch. He'd take two or three short scenes and hand them to his assistant to animate. Then, after he viewed the pencil tests, he turned it into his sequence. He'd make comments, but it removed a lot of pressure because it helped ease me into animation without being assigned under a director.

Q:

©Wdp

To my good friend Jim Korkis
Jack Hannah 4/20/87

ments on *The Woody Woodpecker Show.* He returned to Disney in the Sixties to work as a story consultant on live action films. In 1975, Hannah was asked by the Disney studio to take charge of the Character Animation program at California Institute of the Arts (Cal Arts) located in Valencia, Calif. Now retired, Hannah returned to painting. He is a skilled landscape artist with paintings displayed in galleries throughout the West. The following excerpts are from a series of interviews conducted with Hannah by Jim Korkis from 1977-1990.

Original pencil sketch by Jack Hannah of Donald Duck

Why did you move out of animation into the story department?

A:

When Jack King joined the studio to do a new series of cartoons about Donald Duck, I was picked to join this crew as a full-fledged animator. Even though I worked in this unit for some time, I consider my work at that period of time as "in the middle." I didn't knock 'em dead with my animation, but the director, Jack King, always seemed pleased with what I came up with. About this time, the *Snow White* excitement was stirring up the studio and Walt started looking all over the country for fresh talent. Several "middle-of-the-roaders," like myself, were pegged to be moved aside for some new talent.

At the time, they would hand out scripts of stories looking for story ideas. Anyone could submit gags and we'd be paid anywhere between $2.50 and $5 for each gag that was used. I was turning in a lot of gags and Harry Reeves, who was in charge of the story department, got me transferred over to story. It wasn't as smooth as I make it sound. It really did hurt because I really did love animation, even though I knew I was never going to be one of the top animators.

Q:

How did the story department work in those days?

A:

We'd develop a story with a crew of two storymen. I was teamed with Carl Barks. At certain points, we'd call in two or three other groups for gag ses-

Example of transcript of a story meeting for an unmade Donald Duck cartoon, 1939

© Walt Disney Prod.

sions. It was real teamwork in those sessions. You could either use all or part of what was suggested or just throw it out completely. When we thought the story was ready, we would call Walt Disney in and show him the storyboards. He'd often have little changes to suggest and that would have a domino effect that would make something else happen in the story and then something else. Lots of times, your whole story would change because of that one little idea. Sometimes he'd get real excited and act out those changes right in front of you. He'd be like a kid. He'd crawl on the floor if he had to in order to get a point across. He was really alive when it came to story.

Q:

How did you come up with story ideas for a short?

A:

Carl and I would sit there for two or three days talking over things. Often, we'd go to the library to look through magazines and books for something that would spark an idea. It was always rough, especially after we'd done so many shorts with Donald Duck. It was hard coming up with a new twist. That was the reason new characters, like Chip 'n' Dale, were created. They gave us new springboards for stories.

When we got an idea, Carl and I would hash it over. Carl might start a section and I would try to put a top on it or send it off in a different direction. At some point, I'd take a section and he'd take a section and we'd go to our desks right in the same room and do story sketching, then blocking it out on a board.

Q:

Why did you move into directing?

A:

I was always interested in directing. However, this seemed the right time because Carl left the studio and I was becoming more aware of the fact that Jack King, when he directed our stories, would do them just as we had them on the storyboard. He knew how to put a gag over but paid little attention to personality in Donald Duck. He would very seldom add "touches" that would enhance personality in the character. Personality is the whole key to good animation and a good character. A good animator knows that he doesn't just draw the character; he has to put some personality into the character. Why did actors like Clark Gable or John Wayne become stars? It was not necessarily their great acting. No, it was their personality that made the difference.

Q:

How did you get the chance to move into directing?

A:

There was a young storyman who was having some trouble in the department on his story and I was called in to help. As I worked on it, I felt I could put more personality into it if I directed it myself. Finally, Walt gave in and let me direct *Donald's Off Day* (1944). While I was working on it, the head of the story department came by and told me that Walt said it was okay to pick up another short to direct. I ended up directing cartoons at Disney for 17 years.

Q:

Did you enjoy directing?

A:

Yes, definitely. I liked directing because there was more control. The director has the whole story in mind, the big picture. The director should know the flow and the pacing of the entire thing and why something should or should not be added. An animator only works on his scenes and may decide to add little things, but it is the director who needs to decide whether those elements are going to distract from the main thrust of the story.

Q:

Did you feel your background in story helped you?

A:

Without question. I think the fact that I was a storyman gave me an edge over some other directors. How can someone direct effectively without a good sense of story? I think it's part of a director's job to find areas where he can "plus" a story. I think all animation directors need to have the experience of going through the story department.

Q:

Did you often make changes on stories given to you to direct?

A:

Take *Lambert the Sheepish Lion* (1952) which I think was one of the best things I ever did. It had class. It was a beautiful story. However storymen Bill Peet and Ralph Wright, who were both good storymen, got upset for little things I changed. I never followed a story exactly as it was turned in to me. If I felt I could enhance the story, I changed it but you had to always think of costs. You couldn't be

horsing around and change just for the sake of change. Even in those day, animation was pretty costly. But I knew how they felt because I would have been upset if somebody had changed one of my stories unless I was completely convinced that the change improved the story.

Sometimes I was wrong in making a change. On a Goofy short, Peet complained about a change where I made a spectator raucous and wild where he felt the character should behave just the opposite. After I thought about it, I kind of agreed with him.

Q:

Did previewing the cartoons in theaters help?

A:

We were very conscious of the fact that we were making the cartoon for an audience, not just for ourselves. We'd show the rough reel to an audience of people from ink and paint, even janitors if they were around. They even had cards to fill out about the short. We listened to the reactions closely. When we previewed the short in theaters, we always got a good reaction because we had done our homework. I ran these same shorts for my students when I taught at Cal Arts and the belly laughs are at the same place and the dead spots are at the same place they were many, many years ago. I don't think what I think of my work means a hell of a lot; it's what the audience thinks that counts.

Q:

How is animation different today?

A:

When I was directing shorts, cartoons were fresher to people.

HANNAH

Today, people see animation everywhere. I remember my father telling me one time that the characters in my cartoons moved too fast and that he couldn't understand the dialog. To be honest with you, lately I've seen some new cartoons on television and I have the same feelings he did. I was complaining and my wife said, "You're acting just like your dad did." I just had to laugh because I realized she was right.

Q:

What is the future of animation?

A:

I think the future has never looked brighter for animation. There are so many animated features being made today. You can turn on a TV and can't go more than a half hour without seeing some type of animation. There are jobs everywhere and not just in the entertainment area. I remember a time when Disney was full and you never had a chance of getting in unless you were a genius. When I taught at Cal Arts, I told students to expose themselves to as many aspects of fine arts as possible because they would need that information if they wanted to become the best animators. Many of those students are now at Disney.

Q:

Any closing thoughts?

A:

I like all cartoons, even those I didn't do. Of course, I have a special fondness for the ones I did because, when I look at them today, they bring back other memories of people I worked with and events that were going on and so forth. Animation is a great teamwork thing. I've worked with so many top pros.

So many of those top pros are gone. It's sort of funny in a way. Nobody ever seems old in this business.

Hannah's Humphrey the Bear and Little Ranger from the Disney cartoon shorts

© Walt Disney Prod.

Charles Martin (Chuck) Jones was born in Spokane, Wash., Sept. 21, 1912. His films have received 14 Academy Award nominations and 3 Oscars. After high school graduation, he attended the Chouinard Art Institute. He worked at a variety of jobs including washing cels for Ub Iwerks at Pat Powers' Celebrity Pictures. He worked his way up to an inbetweener before he left the studio. In 1933, he joined the Warner Brothers cartoon division and worked alongside many other talented animation figures, including Tex Avery, Bob Clampett and Friz Freleng. In 1938, he became a director responsible for many memorable cartoons. Jones played a key role in the development of Warner cartoons' style of humor and characters. In particular, along with writer Michael Maltese, he co-created such Warners' stars as the Road Runner and Coyote and Pepe LePew. Jones left Warner in 1963 to head up

Charles M. "Chuck" Jones

Q:

How did you start in animation?

A:

I attended Chouinard Art Institute, now known as California Institute of the Arts, graduating without distinction or the ability to draw. After nearly 10 years of night school with Donald Graham, I still could not draw but I now could fake it quite well. Bad drawing was no particular advantage in the field of commercial art, but it was ideal for celluloid washing.

I got a job with Ub Iwerks, who had just started his own studio after leaving Walt Disney. He was doing the Flip the Frog series. I graduated to inking and then, eventually, inbetweening. Then I went to Walter Lantz for a short time and also Charlie

Mintz. These periods were all very brief. The whole time period at these places was less than two years. I really wasn't sure I wanted to be an animator. I didn't see much future in it. I spent some time doing sketches of people for a dollar apiece on Olvera Street in Los Angeles.

Q:

How did you first join Warners?

A:

I had married Dorothy Webster, who had fired me when I was working at Iwerks. She helped me get a start at Warners in 1933 and I spent the next 28 years there. As an animator, I worked for directors like Jack King and Friz (Freleng). I was working as an inbetweener to Ham Hamilton and he was the

Seventies pencil sketch of that Oscar-winning rabbit by Chuck Jones

© Warner Bros.

one who eased me off in-betweening and into animation. This was on the Buddy series and fortunately nothing in the way of bad animation could make Buddy worse than he was anyway.

Q:
What did you think of the work from the Disney Studio at this time?
A:
We viewed their work with absolute awe. In terms of international communication, Disney was the first one to break through. His cartoons were accepted all over the world. We never considered ourselves in the same league. In many ways, Disney is still the most important man in animation because he created an atmosphere where animators could flourish. In doing

so, he pointed the way for everybody else to animate creatively.

Q:
How did Warners develop so many memorable characters?
A:
Mahler once said his Sixth symphony came to him when he was opening a sandwich and peered down at the greasy wrapping paper. Likewise, there is no "moment of inspiration" for a cartoon character. It is more a process of evolution. In those days, you never set out to create a long-running character. However, when you found a personality that worked, you'd begin thinking of ways to build upon it. Whenever we would begin using a character on a regular basis, rules would soon be developed. These were the "givens" that

MGM's animation division. There he directed a series of Tom and Jerry cartoons. More noteworthy was his MGM work on unusual shorts like the award winning The Dot and the Line, the TV special How the Grinch Stole Christmas, and the feature film, The Phantom Tollbooth. For a year, Jones was vice-president of the ABC-TV network assigned to children's programming. His major project was a Saturday morning show entitled Curiosity Shop. Eventually, he established his own independent production company, responsible for many half hour animated TV specials including Rikki Tikki Tavi and The Cricket in Times Square. In recent years, he has returned to working on the classic Warner characters in theatrical and TV projects starring Bugs Bunny and Daffy Duck. In 1990, Jones announced establishment of a new independent production company. The following excerpts are from various question and answer sessions, attended by Jim Korkis between 1968-1990.

Original pencil sketch of Daffy Duck Dodgers, 1983

© Warner Bros.

could not be broken and still have character maintained. And that was the key to so many of the Warner characters. They weren't funny because of the way they were drawn; they were funny because of what they did and how they did things. It is the ability of the character's personality to have an attitude that is funny.

Q:
Did you receive support from the Warners executives?
A:
A classic Eddie Selzer [a top executive at Warner] story was when he came in one day and we were just sitting around talking and laughing. He was just fuming in the doorway and said, "What the hell has all this laughter got to do with the making of animated cartoons?" That was one of his classic lines.

Q:
How helpful was it to work with the same team at Warners?
A:
The team thing is very important. It gets to the point where you can snap your fingers, or make a single drawing to convey your idea. Whenever a new animator came to work for me, he was in trouble for a while, because on my exposure sheets, I would put down "BAL" which meant "balance" or "ANT" which meant "anticipate." And all my animators had to know exactly what they meant. I'd want a particular character balanced solid on his feet before he did something. We began to understand that we could anticipate by one frame. If a step is supposed to come down on a beat, we found out that if you move it up one frame, it would work, would make the step appear to be exactly on beat. We found it worked best for the entire theater if you were one frame ahead of the beat.

Q:

What is important in animation?

A:

Occasionally an artist should look at his tools and ask himself what he cannot do without, the essentials — what he *must* have to pursue his form of expression in animation. He *must* have only three things—a pencil, a number of sheets of paper and a light source. With these he can animate; without them he cannot. All other additions are conveniences and embellishments which shade his art form toward others. He does not even need a motion picture camera. The first valid animation, indeed the first motion pictures, were without such cameras. One of the odd misunderstandings about animation even by those who work in the field is that an individual drawing has the same importance as an illustration. Animation is a chorus of drawings working in tandem, each contributing a part to the whole of a time/space idea. If a single drawing, as a drawing, dominates the action, it is probably bad animation, even though it may be a good drawing.

Q:

As a director, do you try to keep an audience in mind when working?

A:

Only in my first year or two as a director did I try to figure out what the public wanted and try to supply that want. Then I discovered that the public hasn't any idea at all what it wants, as was so appallingly proved in the case of the Edsel automobile, in which the Ford automobile company spent a reported quarter of a billion dollars trying to build an automobile to the public's taste, and the public's taste came out looking, as Bob Hope put it, "like a Buick sucking a lemon."

What I have tried to do always was to realize that my field was laughter, that I should never make a film without trying something new, that something should never be ostentatious, and that I should always put in something just for myself. That I should live within, without being inhibited by, the commercial limitations of my position. That I should ignore what the public wants without once ignoring the public. Above all, that I must never underestimate the public. And finally, I must remember that eight to 10 hours of every day was a big portion of my life and what I did during that time should be happy and stimulating.

Q:

Why do you continue to produce animation?

A:

In my opinion, and only for myself and this is a very personal statement, the most rewarding place to work is out in the public theatrical arena, where all directors, writers, actors seem to find their greatest satisfaction. Animation is not only an art form, but a means of communication as well, and at the risk of shocking the purists, a means of mass communication as well. A matador, a ballet dancer, a violinist all have to eventually meet the public, usually en masse. I have no idea who that public is, what they want, how they function, or what they would look like in a cross section. But the kind of animated comedy that I enjoy most requires public acceptability.

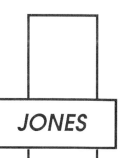

JONES

Chuck Jones' demonstration, in 1974, of the difference between full animation and television's limited animation

Q:

How would you define animation?

A:

Animation, as I understand it, is the art of the impossible. The only art form yet designed that can create from whole cloth, or whole paper, a form of life never seen before, to resurrect a form long dead, or to anticipate the possibilities of new life, or the future of life in reality, or in man's mind. Distortion and oddity alone are not enough to make a good animated film.

A recent article on animation speaks of "modern" animation as freeing the animator from the chains that bind him to his drawing board. What a strange idea! What artist wants to be freed from his drawing board? What most of us want is to escape the terrible trivialities and duties that keep us from our drawing boards. All of us here who came in after 1935 inherited a world where animation was accepted, beloved and commercially able to support us. Walt Lantz, Dave Fleischer, Bill Nolan, Grim Natwick, Ub Iwerks, etc., etc. and above all, Walt Disney, were the men who did this for us. We live and flourish in the ground they prepared.

Q:

What should beginning animators keep in mind?

A:

Fundamentals. Not a return to fundamentals but an awareness of fundamentals. "Fundamentals," as I use the word here, are what learning to write is to letters. How to write and what tools you need to write, not what to write about or what opinion to express or whether you write on black velvet with charcoal. Fundamentals are the tools that en-able a violinist to recognize that there are strings on a violin and that you usually stick it under your chin and not up your shirt sleeve—that there are keys and scales and other useful things.

Fundamentals are the recognition of the basic needs of the animation craft—color, perhaps, a lens, maybe. Paper, yes. Control, yes. Imagination, yes—and a pencil, a ream of paper, about 10 years of good draftsmanship practice and the realization that anything—anything—is possible with a moving line—if you know how. No great animator spent less than 10 years to achieve the facility that will enable them to do for instance what a pianist must do to perform without worrying where his fingers are.

Q:

Why do you call "animator" a "gift word?"

A:

I have always been a little itchy about the use of "art" and "artist" as a self-applied appellation. The "gift word" anecdote is one I've told many times. A young man was once sent from Columbia University with a mutual friend's introduction to the great poet, Robert Frost. Frost looked at the young man's writings and then asked, "What do you do, son?" The young man drew himself up proudly and said, "I am a poet!" Frost gently answered, "The term 'poet' is a gift word son, you cannot give it to yourself." The terms "animator" or "artist" are gift words, too, and yet they are employed as self-description by an amazing number of people.

Bill Scott, born in Philadelphia in 1920, worked as an animation writer and producer for more than 40 years, including 27 years at the Jay Ward Studio. When he enlisted in the Air Force in 1942, he was assigned to an animation unit where he found himself washing cels, doing in-betweening and, eventually, layout work. After his discharge, he worked for a short time as a storyman at Warner Brothers. He went on to do story work for other productions including Bob Clampett's Time for Beany, a TV puppet show. He did writing as well as some puppet work and voices. He next joined a group known as Industrial Films, which became United Productions of America (UPA). While there he was involved in co-writing the award-winning short, Gerald McBoing-Boing and being associate producer of the Gerald McBoing-Boing Show for TV. It was Scott who was responsible for the animated adaptation of The Tell Tale Heart. Scott then joined John Su

Bill Scott

Q:

How did you get interested in animation?

A:

I was always interested in animation. In Colorado when I was about 18 or 19, I hooked up with this guy who had actually built himself a homemade multiplane camera, if you imagine such a thing. He and I worked for one summer just animating some scenes, pencil animation, to use this cockamamie thing. We loved animation. We would read the credits on all the cartoons and knew names like Phil Monroe.

Q:

How did you get into an animation unit during World War II?

A:

I was supposed to be assigned to a combat camera crew, but I was in a play that Special Services was doing so I was put on detached service. When the play finished, I reported to where my unit was supposed to be at Culver City and I discovered that there was an animation unit there. The commanding officer was Rudy Ising and when I explained my background to him, I got transferred into the unit.

I started out washing cels, because they were scarce at that time and you had to re-use them. You really can't get lower than washing cels. I spent my spare time trying to learn how to draw. How to trace, actually. I became an inker for a while, but they brought in some girls to do that so they tried me as an inbetweener. Then I got moved up and I was an assistant animator to

42

greetin's and thanx to Jim from Bullwinkle and *Bill Scott*

therland Productions, where he wrote many industrial films for big business. When he left, he freelanced as a writer for TV commercials for two years until in 1958, he was introduced to Jay Ward and eventually the two men became partners. They were responsible for Rocky and His Friends, The Bullwinkle Show, Fractured Flickers, The George of the Jungle Show, and many other classic projects like commercials for cereals such as Captain Crunch.

In addition to being a writer, Scott supplied many of the voices for characters like Bullwinkle and Dudley Do-Right. Shortly before his death in 1985, he had been doing voice work for The Gummi Bears. Scott also served as President of ASIFA-Hollywood for many years. The following excerpts are from an interview with Scott conducted by Jim Korkis in 1982.

people like Bill Hurtz and Phil Monroe. These were superb draftsmen and great animators and I'm trying to scratch the breakdown drawings for them. They were both very nice and they'd cover up my mistakes for me and they'd do the work when I couldn't do it and so forth.

Q:
So you weren't a good artist?
A:
I can't drawn worth a damn. I was still at the point where I'd have to hold stuff up to a mirror to see if it was true or not. The one thing that saved me was that when anything happened that was the least bit humorous or notable, a whole series of gags would start about it. Little panel gags would be handed around and everyone would laugh. I

couldn't draw worth a pinch, but I was good enough to draw these funny ideas about situations and would drop them on people's desks and they'd just laugh and laugh and pass them around. I think that's the real reason I lasted as long as I did there.

Q:
After the service, how did you become a storyman at Warners?
A:
Bob Clampett had left a short time before and they had promoted an animator named Art Davis to the post of director. They were looking for some new storymen for this unit. So they hired a fellow named Lloyd Turner and me. I was working with my heroes. They were all guys I'd heard about for so long. As far as I was concerned they

Greetings from Bill Scott and Bullwinkle

© Jay Ward

were the greatest writers in the business. Names like Mike Maltese, Tedd Pierce and Warren Foster.

Q:

How did you go about creating a story?

A:

Those guys could produce really remarkable stuff. It used to be that you'd start each story with a blank piece of cellotex on your wall. It was four by eight, I remember. I think it was Mike Maltese one time drew a huge mouth on his and it said "AL-WAYS HUNGRY!" You'd start doing little pieces of story and pinned them up. When you got enough pinned up to run seven minutes you were finished.

Q:

And it took about six weeks to do that?

A:

One occasion, Mike Maltese was working with another story-man and he just got a flash of an idea and he wrote this whole bloody story in less than a week. The other story guy was right with him sketching like mad. They had finished this story in a week but they didn't put it up in a week. All the sketches were shoved in the drawer and they goofed around and threw push pins and told stories and snuck out to lunch and all that. At the end of each day, they'd pull out a handful of sketches, pin 'em up and it took exactly six weeks to do this story.

Q:

Do you think the background you had animating helped as a storyman?

A:

Of course. A good animation

writer needs to have an awareness of the medium, what is capable of being done. It's also useful to know how to draw. It's not vital. There are some writers who can't draw worth a darn but it is easier to sketch out little stick figures than type a page and a half of instructions and directions. I also developed a sense of animation timing, how long a scene should be to work for an audience.

Q:

Was writing at UPA different than at Warners?

A:

To begin with, you *never* mentioned Warners! The kiss of death at UPA was to be considered a Warner Brothers writer. They were considered clothesline gag people with lots of violence. At UPA, you had to be able to justify your humor, which was difficult to do. You couldn't write a big blow-off for your joke and pay it off with a big animation tag, or a pose. They wouldn't let you do it. It was much more cerebral. It was only with Magoo, because he was such an outrageous character, that I could use some of the wilder aspects of animation. It was also tough because very few of the directors were really well-versed in story. They would know what they liked but they couldn't tell you until they saw it. I never got to go along to any of the previews because I was *only* a writer. Writers were still pretty low on the totem pole.

Q:

Was that true at all studios?

A:

Writers in the early days of animation, and even today at some places, were considered, at best, a necessary evil. In some ways, I dislike the term "story-man." We're writers. But I guess being a "storyman" is better than being a "gag man" which is a term that lasted into the Forties.

for longer films you need to get involved with the character more. The character should change from the beginning of the picture. Something should have happened that has made him different

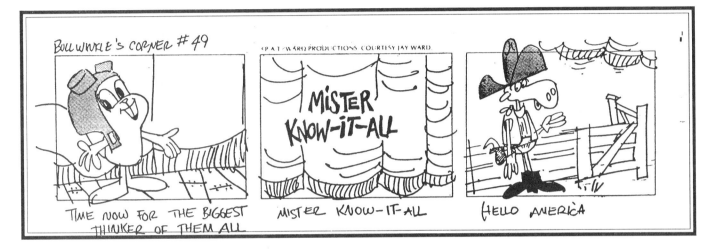

BULLWINKLE'S CORNER #49

TIME NOW FOR THE BIGGEST THINKER OF THEM ALL

(P A T WARD PRODUCTIONS COURTESY JAY WARD)

MISTER KNOW-IT-ALL

MISTER KNOW-IT-ALL

HELLO AMERICA

People could earn extra income by turning in gags for a cartoon. One of these days, people in animation are going to admit that writing is of prime importance. It's writers who go about inventing the worlds that never previously existed.

Q:

What is the most important thing an animation writer should know?

A:

A writer needs to know how to tell a story. It's not as easy as it sounds. There is a basic structure that writers need to understand. The story needs to start with something that is going to grab the audience's interest. The story continues through incidents that enlarge on that idea. The tension needs to keep increasing steadily. Then there should be a climax and a period of release. I guess you'd say that the pattern is to go up gradually and to come quickly down. Plays are like that. Novels are like that. Of course,

somehow, like seeing things differently.

Q:

So an animated film is similar to a play?

A:

Drawings can't act. Actors act. Although there are similarities, there are important differences. Animation is more compressed. You can communicate information in three or four minutes that it might take a real person an hour or more to do. Cartoons aren't real; they are caricatures. You can still get a strong emotional reaction from an audience using caricatures if you know what you are doing.

Q:

Would it be difficult to write a good animated feature?

A:

It's very difficult to write anything good for animation. Because animation itself is such a powerful medium that it just gobbles up material. A scene which

Storyboard from "Mr. Know-it-all" segment of THE BULLWINKLE SHOW

© Jay Ward

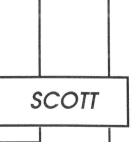

SCOTT

would last in a live action movie maybe a minute or so would be done in animation in 10 seconds. I would assume that the equivalent of writing a reasonable animation feature would be three or four features in live action as far as the material is concerned. An animation writer has to do it all. He can't just say, "Well, this is an Eddie Murphy part so Eddie Murphy will do something funny with this material." No, once the writer is finished, the animator is going to have to dream up the business, dream up the scenes, etc. that could make the thing work. But if you don't give the animator a strong story, if you don't give him something that is really going to inspire him, or hang on to, then the whole thing is lost.

Q:

What is your greatest concern about animation in general?

A:

Right now, I would say that it seems to me that there is almost nowhere for anybody to become very good at any one phase of animation. I don't think the man exists who is going to be a nonpareil writer, designer, animator. I think those three areas really require three different kinds of thinking, skills and aptitude. I see a lot of people employed in animation. I find very few people who are proud of what they are doing. In some ways, I think we've produced a generation of people who do second-rate story work, second-rate design and second-rate animation not because they don't want to be any better, but because they can make a living doing what they are doing. There's no opportunity nor motivation to learn, or to use your expertise.

Q:

What advice would you give to someone wanting to write for animation?

A:

Read. Read. And read some more. Ready anything and everything. Join a drama group. Get up on stage and see what works for an audience. There are no writers trained in dramaturgy who are also trained in animation. I said to my wife the other day that if I'd known how things were going to be when I was 62 years old, I would have gone to a lot more screenwriting classes. I would have written a lot more live action projects. That writing would have prepared me to write a really good animated feature.

Q:

Any closing thoughts?

A:

Why is the most powerful and effective medium for communicating ideas, emotions, abstract concepts and sheer fun not reaching an audience? What gives me hope is that there are people who'll work long hours for little or no money just to make an animated cartoon. I know people personally who spend their own money and time and bust their buns just to do an animated cartoon to have done an animated cartoon. For myself, I still love animation, which is funny because lately I've seen very little animation which is funny. I'm glad I had the opportunity to work in animation. I had fun.

DUDLEY DO-RIGHT OF THE MOUNTIES

NARRATOR: SNIDELY WHIPLASH, THAT SCANDALOUS, NEFARIOUS, ODIOUS, OBNOXIOUS, VILLIANOUS, VILLIAN OF THE NORTHWEST HAD OUT DONE HIMSELF. HE HAD BECOME SO SHOCKINGLY DESPICABLE THAT HE COULDN'T STAND HIMSELF.

SNIDELY: YOU ARE ROTTEN TO THE CORE, SNIDELY WHIPLASH, ROTTEN, ROTTEN, ROTTEN! HOW DID I EVER GET STARTED TYING LADIES TO RAILROAD TRACKS. IF I COULD ONLY STOP...BUT I CAN'T STOP...I'VE GOT THIS THING!

(RCMP CAMP)

INSPECTOR: I'VE ALWAYS TOLD YOU, DUDLEY, THAT SNIDELY WHIP-LASH WAS A "BAD EGG".

DUDLEY: YES YOU HAVE, INSPECTOR!

INSPECTOR: WELL HE'S BEYOND HELP NOW. I THOUGHT IF WE COULD "BRING HIM IN" IN TIME WE COULD SET HIM ON THE RIGHT PATH... SHOW HIM THAT TYING LADIES TO RAIL-ROAD TRACKS IS NOT THE CANADIAN WAY.

DUDLEY: WE MUSN'T GIVE UP HOPE, SIR.

INSPECTOR: NO, DUDLEY, WE MUST CATCH HIM AND PUT HIM AWAY FROM SOCIETY. SNIDELY WHIPLASH IS IRREFORMABLE!

DUDLEY: THAT'S PRETTY STRONG TALK, SIR.

INSPECTOR: BUT MY HANDS HAVEN'T BEEN IDLE, DUDLEY. I HAVE INVENTED...A "SNIDELY-CATCHING MACHINE."

DUDLEY: AND IT'S A BEAUTY. UH, HOW DOES IT WORK, INSPEC-TOR?

INSPECTOR: WELL, YOU SEE THIS DUMMY WOMAN HERE NEXT TO THE RAILROAD TRACKS?

DUDLEY: YES.

INSPECTOR: WELL SNIDELY ISN'T GOING TO BE ABLE TO RESIST TRYING TO TIE HER TO THE RAILROAD TRACKS...HE HAS A "THING" ABOUT THAT.

DUDLEY: SO WHAT WILL HAPPEN?

INSPECTOR: TRY IT DUDLEY.

DUDLEY: ALL-RIGHT...

(Dudley grabs for girl. Arm grabs Dudley and he ends up caught in cage. Nell enters)

SCOTT

Animation Today: The Interviews

The artists who made theatrical shorts in animation's "Golden Age" never worried about ratings or box-office or minority pressure groups. Cartoons, newsreels, short subjects, etc. were given to audiences as a bonus with the main feature film. As long as the cartoons came in on time and on budget, few studio executives gave them much thought.

With the entrance into the television market of the Fifties (and to the same extent theatrical features), animation had to actively compete with live action entertainment. Suddenly budgets, time schedules, ratings, box office and other business elements began to become more important. Animation now had to turn a profit.

Many of the newer animation companies no longer were associated with the cash-fat movie studios which began closing their animation studios by the Sixties. A year or two of low-rated shows, a bad theatrical box office, no sale of a new show and a host of other factors could close an entire studio quickly and permanently.

These newer studios often couldn't afford large facilities to house the many workers needed to produce animation. This created a burgeoning freelance talent pool. Many artists worked at home on a variety of projects and only went to the studio to pick up or drop off work.

TV was a seasonal business and animation production followed a similar schedule. Studios would have plenty of work in the Spring and Summer, producing shows for the Fall. Once complete, the studios would have no work for many months, except for those in development or clerical positions. Hundreds of artists might be laid off and forced to find other sources of income before the new hiring season began.

In an effort to supply new animation cheaply, some producers purchased shows produced in other countries. Eventually the producers began sending the work overseas, where labor costs were low. This created the loss of many jobs. Ironically, one of those jobs was the actual task of animating. The only major animation still being done in the U.S. was in the occasional animated special and TV commercials.

While the animation industry was spiraling further downward, the public perception of animation also was being lowered. No longer considered entertainment

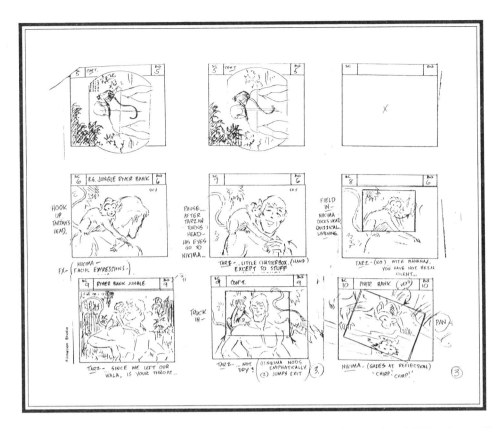

for audiences of all ages, animation became fully labeled a children's medium, primarily because animation on television served effectively as an electronic baby-sitter.

In the late Seventies, animation began to rise from the ashes, like a phoenix. TV animation began to improve as writers tried new directions. The many foreign studios were now doing better work. A new re-birth in the financial success of features created interest in that area. By the late Eighties, a new "animation boom" had begun that continues in full force today.

New trends were established. One of the most disturbing new directions was the desire for ever-shortening deadlines. Features previously took several years to create; new features were expected to be done in a year or less. Saturday morning shows were given less than six months to go from development to airing.

Work was everywhere, but many artists had to work long hours more frequently. It was not unusual for studios to demand regular overtime during productions and to restrict time off and vacations. The shortage of talent caused some studios to put staff members under contracts, which at times only prevent the talent from quitting but allows the studio to lay off talent at any time.

The increased output makes it more difficult to find enough time slots for animation to be seen. Usually early morning and late afternoon time periods are the only blocks of time set aside for animated shows. Despite the many cable and independent stations, there are only a limited number of hours for an increasing slate of new and returning shows.

TV producers fight for the best time slots and recently attempted to create groups of shows to air in a particular order to lock out competition. Theatrical releases need to be strategically planned for maximum initial box office. Just like a live action blockbuster, if an animated feature premieres and does not do as well as "planned" on the opening weekend, it will be considered a failure and quickly disappear from theaters.

Security at studios also is being continuously upgraded. Some studios will not allow employees of other studios into their facilities, due to the increased fear that a project will be "stolen."

Today's animation industry is far different than it was even a few years ago. In an effort to give as accurate an account of the current industry as possible, we interviewed the following 16 professionals. These creators range from "new talent" (but all have at least eight years in the business) to "golden age" veterans who are still active in the business. In an effort to supply the widest range of industry information, we interviewed creators who work (and have worked) at many different studios. All 16 interviewees are known among their peers as craftsmen in their field, although they may be unknown to the general public.

Though the interview lengths vary, there was no favoritism given on the part of the authors. Interviewees were asked similar questions relating to their career, the job they do, their routine and what they would recommend new artists do to get into the business. Those in the same field/job were asked identical questions. All interviews were restricted to no more than one hour in length.

Some interviewees used their time simply to answer the questions; others used the questions and comments as springboards for comments and examples. All were given the rough transcription to edit out topics and lines they felt inappropriate. This process did cause some interviews to be shortened dramatically, and some questions dropped. The interviews then were lightly edited for clarity and grammar. We have attempted to maintain as much of the personality of the interviewee as possible.

Illustrations in the interviews are examples of the work of the interviewee. The number and quality of samples vary by interviewee due to their (and the authors') access to materials.

We wish to thank these talented creators for allowing us to talk with them and appearing in this book.

Opposite: Part of the storyboard, by Mitch Schauer, of the opening title sequence from BOBBY'S WORLD © *Film Roman*

This page: Roger Rabbit preliminary character design from 1982 by Chris Buck. © *Walt Disney*

PROD. #

FILM ROMAN

PAGE 11

(SC. 5 CONT'D.) ——— PAN ➔

(SC. 5 CONT'D.) ——— PAN ➔

(SC. 5 CONT'D.) ——— PAN ➔

(5 CONT'D.)

CAPTAIN SQUASH FLIES IN A LOOP AROUND BOBBY. BOBBY WAVES TO HIS FAVORITE HERO.

(CAPTAIN SQUASH CONTINUES HIS "CORK SCREW" AROUND BOBBY. BOBBY LOOKS OVER THE SIDE OF HIS SHIP TO WATCH THE HERO.

BOBBY'S SHIP IS BEGINNING TO ROLL TO HIS LEFT.

AS BOBBY BANKS HIS SHIP UP INTO CAMERA, CAPT. SQUASH STREAKS DOWNWARD BEHIND THE VEHICLE.

THE BODY OF BOBBY'S SHIP FILLS THE SCREEN.

Pete Alvarado

DATE: AUGUST 27, 1990

Q:
*Can you give me a brief de-
scription of your career including studios you've worked
for and specific productions
you've worked on?*

A:
Well, let me see. I might as
well start with Disney because
that goes back to 1937 and the
tail end of *Snow White*. I didn't
stick around Disney's too long. I
went on to Warner Brothers and
other places. I went back to Disney briefly for a few months during *Dumbo*, but it didn't seem to
click. Then, there was a period
where I went with MGM.

I was doing basic animation
like inbetweening and the nuts
and bolts; learning the thing from
the ground up. Everyone, at that

time, had to pay their dues and
put in their apprenticeship. Some
places had what they called "the
bullpen." Everyone would do basically the same things, clean up
and inbetween or whatever was
required, and it was pretty tedious stuff, and I was very happy
to get out of it (laughs). Most of
the guys were.

Anyway, that was something
that everyone seemed to have to
do, at that time before they
branched out into the other spe-
cialties. Fundamentally, I was
doing animation although I was
always leaning toward wherever
I could try to find out where they
were doing the story sketches or
backgrounds or more creative
stuff like character design—that
kind of thing.

My training in art school was
fine arts. It being the Depression,

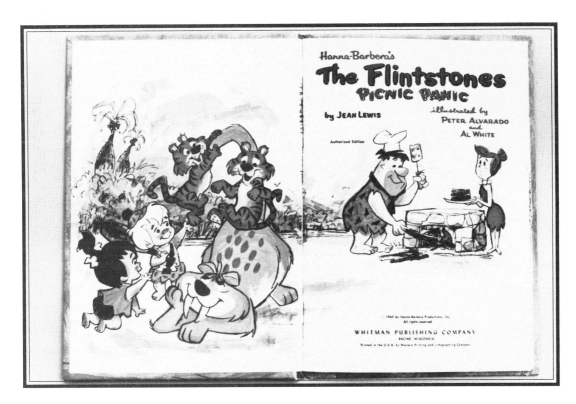

Inside a Whitman BIG Tell-a-Tale

most of us in the art school were thinking about making a living with our art. At that time, Disney was the big employer in town. And so that's why most of the talent in the art school ended up with Disney's, at least for a while.

My first tour at Warner's was the black and white Bob Clampett unit, doing the Porky Pigs and stuff like that. This is before World War Two, of course. I then moved to MGM and worked with Hanna and Barbera. They allowed me to do some assistant layout work with Harvey Eisenberg (Jerry Eisenberg's father). He was doing the Tom and Jerrys at that time. Hanna and Barbera were looking around for artists that could replace him because Harvey was thinking of moving to the Barney Google comic strip. The strip's artist, Billy De Beck, was ill and the syndicate was looking for artists. Harvey tried out, but he was eventually turned down, although he was a superb artist. Actually, it was very flattering to be thought of as a replacement for him.

Then I had a hiatus in the service for a couple of years, and upon coming back, I decided I was going to try to really get into the more creative end of the business. From that point, I really slanted more toward layout, character design, that type of thing, and background painting.

Then my second stint at Warner's began. It was interesting. I happened to hit at a time when Chuck Jones was in a period where he produced a lot of very, very good films. He had a lot of talented people working for him at the time. I considered it really a stroke of luck (laughs) to be with them. There were top people like Tedd Pierce and Mike Maltese and Warren Foster; an-

the talent around you is so good, you have to hit for a higher level of quality, and I think that had a lot to do with it. We did a lot of films and things like the Road Runner and Pepe Le Pew and,

Background from RABBIT HOOD (Warner Brothers)

© Warner Brothers

imators like Ken Harris, Ben Washam, Abe Levitow. I really enjoyed working with Chuck, and there were men like Bob Givens, also. Well, I had known Bob before in the old days of black and white, before World War Two, but we became reacquainted with the Jones unit.

We created a lot of new characters and it was just a very prolific period for everybody. I'd say it was one of those unique situations where people would spin off of one another. Because

oh, you could name a slew of them.

I then heard that Western Publishing was coming out to the [West] coast. They were setting up an office out in Beverly Hills, and looking for artists. They had Carl Barks, one of the first ones they hired, and then, Jesse Marsh from Disney. With Western Publishing, I ran into an interesting thing. They offered contracts which, at the time, were unheard of in the animation business. So I grabbed it. I began to divide my time between the studios and Western, doing books. They not only did comic books, but the Little Golden Books and all kinds of games and puzzles and you name it. I did that until Western went out of business (laughs). Well, they're still in business, more or less. But I do it by mail now to the East Coast. I guess you can say I was just about the last contract artist Western had until they closed their L.A. office.

I was soon doing a lot of work for Hanna-Barbera, particularly layout and character drawing, stuff like that, for *The Jetsons, Yogi Bear*, and *The Flintstones*. I would wear two hats (laughs). I had six months at the studios and six months of books. I did that for a lot of years. I also did a lot of burning the night oil. But it worked out pretty well because of the way the television season worked. The studios would phase out around September or October, and that was just about the time I'd start doing my books.

I also worked at other studios. I worked for Bakshi-Krantz on the daring *Fritz the Cat, Nine Lives of Fritz the Cat*. There were periods with DePatie-Freleng when they were doing different kinds of shows like the *Pink Panther* and other things. I kind of alternated between whoever was busiest. But I would basically say Hanna-Barbera, for many years, was pretty much one of my base studios that I did a lot of work for.

Q:

When did you get into actual storyboarding?

A:

I guess I did some in the '50s. I really got into boarding with television. I got my feet wet do-

ing just spec stuff. I began to board a little later on, after they'd run out of layout work or something like that. Or maybe I'd start the boards and then eventually work into the layout. When all the runaway production stuff started, then I really seriously thought about storyboarding to fill the gap. With all my training in layout and other things, I figured that I should be able to handle boards. Of course, comic books were good training, too, learning how to stage stuff in a given area quickly and simply.

I always felt storyboarding was such a highly specialized type of thing. The men I knew were men who worked on Disney features and that kind of thing. I admired these guys. To be a good animation story man, you have to have a special something, I don't know what it is, besides being an artist or a writer. I always felt frustrated. The ability to write and draw a storyboard is more satisfying than just drawing it.

Q:

What was your art training?

A:

I had a scholarship at Chouinard's at the time. They're no longer in existence. I guess you could say Cal Arts was the outgrowth of Chouinard. Mrs. Chouinard was a terrific woman, [she] loved her students. During the period I was there, Disney came in and assisted the school financially. It gave them an in to her most talented students. It was a great way to find talent when you think about it. And, of course, the students didn't feel too badly because jobs were kind of scarce, and Disney's was a good way to go.

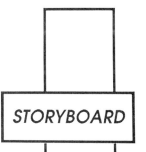

STORYBOARD

Q:

Is that basically how you broke in, by going that way?

A:

Yeah. Like I say, Chouinard taught an animation class, and a lot, maybe 95 percent or more, of the students who went into the class immediately went over to Disney's when they finished. So, it was almost like a Disney training school. Then Disney, himself, had classes going at his studio. So, we were constantly learning. We were training on the job. It was kind of a good era, in a way. Unlike a lot of the studios today, they actually considered it very important. In order to have a pool of trained talent, they would go to the expense of training them themselves if they had to. So (laughs) that's unique. Disney paid people while they learned. I don't know why one of the producers today doesn't break out and do that. If you really want trained talent, train them your way.

Q:

What does a storyboard artist do?

A:

The way I approach it is you've got an animation script. You've got a fundamental story line maybe with gags interspersed or something like that. I think that I've always approached it like an underlying story, and then try to put some acting into the character. Make the characters act, make them breathe, if you can. Like when you do layout and do characters, you try to put a little life into the thing.

I think a lot of fellows just crank out panels. They don't mean anything. And I think a lot of times, it's my belief anyway, that if you put something into the board that has a lot of guts, a good animator will pick up on it. I know this to be true because of the fellows I've worked with. They've mentioned back to me that they like the board I gave them because it kicked them off on something. They had fun and stuff came out looking good, better than it would have.

I'll never forget one time I was talking to Friz Freleng about it. I said, "Gee, do you think we're wasting our time, making nice looking drawings on the board?" He said, "Well, look at it this way, in television, as it goes down the line, it loses. It gets less and less. Everything you put in up front will mean something." In other words, it'll be much better than it would have been. It's a good philosophy, really.

I think you should have a little fun or pride in what you do, and maybe have a little fun with it. But, go at it with some kind of pattern. Even if a lot of times you get a lousy script, and you say, "Gee, this is terrible." The challenge is: what can I do to make it better than it is, or better than it deserves (laughs)? And sometimes, occasionally, you can come up with something extremely funny. One little bit, out of a whole half hour maybe, will be a belly laugh. People will remember it. They'll say, "Gee, who did that funny thing?" It's just a few seconds, but it's so well done, it comes like a shock (laughs).

It's the same with all other art work. Say an ad agency gives you something, and it's a campaign that's dull. What can you do to make it better than it is? Can you liven it up? What can you do to get an audience to look at it? That's the whole thing.

How do you grab the audience? Or how do you make somebody stop and look and listen. I don't think it's anything earthshaking. I think we're entertaining. Maybe some day we'll get into messages, I don't know (laughs). But, right now, I think we're entertaining.

If you can inject a message painlessly, well, fine. That's good. It doesn't hurt. But I think, to entertain, try to take each board you get and inject something into it that'll liven it up or will grab the audience. There's a lot of things you can do, a funny attitude or maybe the way you build up the personality of a character.

Q:
When do you usually get involved with a project?
A:
Well, as a rule, they call you and they say, "We've got this series coming up and we've got X number of shows," or whatever.

They usually have their outlines, but most of the time, (laughs) I don't pay too much attention to them. I wait until after I do a few of the scripts, then I get a feel for the characters and the story line and the flavor that they want. I think a lot of times, they do them so fast, that the men that create them don't realize, the potential until they actually see it on the air.

Q:
How much assistance do you get from the director or the writer?
A:
Well, it depends on the director, the writer. I've found in recent years some of the fellows can be kind of hard-nosed. They have certain ways of doing things, and certain directors wanted to see certain things. Every time, you'd have to prove yourself, or something. Then, other directors were very good about letting you have your free-

STORYBOARD

dom. They would hope you'd come up with something clever, unique, or different, or new, or something like that. Each one seemed to be a little bit different from the other. So, I would say they really aren't all the same, they're just (laughs) human beings that react. Some men in the business don't find anything funny (laughs). Then, I know there are other men who will laugh at every gag no matter how bad it is (laughs).

Q:

What is your daily routine like as a storyboard artist?

A:

Well, I used to be a nine-to-five guy, but I've somehow gotten into a lot of night work where things are quiet, so I just shift my hours. I do, basically, the same number of hours, or maybe even a few more. But, I find that a lot of times at night, without any phones ringing or other things to interrupt, I get a lot more done. I can operate on a very small amount of sleep, so I'm fortunate that way.

I would say I put in my eight hours or more, at least eight hours, and I sit there, and even when something doesn't feel like it's going to work, I just sit there and keep drawing until it does. I don't wait to be inspired. But, occasionally, there are times when I'll go back and maybe look at some of my fine art books or other things, or get a good novel or a good piece of literature or something; get a little change of pace and then come back to my work refreshed.

Q:

Do you use any reference or a lot of reference in your work?

A:

Yes, I have my own personal file for my reference. Over the years, I've had a lot of material that I've used, and I constantly refer back to that. I do surround myself with a lot of reference. So, that probably gets injected into the work, too.

Q:

One thing you hear a lot is that storyboards are sort of like comic books or comic strips. That's often a simplified way of describing it. You've worked in both. Can you say that it is an accurate description?

A:

Well, one art director at Western mentioned that I could adapt easily, but I found that I thought of the two things as separate media. A comic strip is a separate thing from an animation storyboard. I always think of an animation storyboard drawing from the standpoint of layout or animation, that kind of thing. I'm always thinking: what will the animator do with this? What will the layout person do with this? Can they take this and can they build on it, or something like that?

The comic strips and comic books, I recall mainly: How can I eliminate characters (laughs) and make close-ups? Or how many silhouettes can I get to a page (laughs)? I think a lot of us in the business had a few laughs about that. They finally did restrict us to one silhouette a page (laughs). Contrary to what you see today in comic books, where they're usually loaded, we actually kept them relatively simple. We put in crowds and things if it really helped the story, but not as a general rule. We would try interesting angles, we didn't just load it up for the sake of loading it up. I think that's why a lot of those old Dell comics look so good. They were thought through from a story standpoint.

I never treated a comic book script the same as I would an animation script when I board them. They're just not the same. They're two different media. There was an interesting experiment. I can't recall the company that did it, but they tried to blow up comic book panels, and thought they would save a lot of drawing and work, just blowing them up. It just never worked. No matter what they did, it just didn't blow up properly. In other words, they're just two separate media, really.

Q:

What project or film or show or something that you've worked on, has given you the most professional enjoyment or satisfaction and why?

A:

I would say my experience at Warner Brothers was kind of special because of all the talented guys, even when we didn't agree on everything. In fact, we did a lot of disagreeing. All of us were really concerned with what was on the screen, and we were all very professional. They did give us a certain kind of freedom. We had a certain schedule to adhere to, but we could adjust that to fit our own way of working. If you had a five week schedule, that's about what we had roughly to do lay-outs or background. And actually, we could do it much faster most of the time. We'd use that extra time to put little things into the film or maybe save it for another film we wanted to put a few more hours of thinking on or try to improve it. But it was a

good time for me because it was one of the rare times when I always looked forward to going to work (laughs). I guess it wasn't all that perfect, but time's probably mellowed me (laughs).

Q:

A project, on the opposite side, that failed, in your opinion. It may have been a commercial success, but you personally felt did not live up to your expectations.

A:

Well, I was going to say *Rock Odyssey*. I had a lot of hope for that. I think we did a lot of nice work on that thing, but it just never seemed to get off the ground. I think most of us in the business are so close to these things, we don't really know sometimes when we have something.

Q:

And the final question now: if you were to start in the business today, or to offer advice to someone starting in the business today, what would you tell them?

A:

Well, by all means, I would say get as much art schooling as you can, or expose yourself to as many good teachers, whether they're animation people or otherwise. First of all, get yourself a broad, well-rounded knowledge of art, generally, then specialize, if you want, in animation.

Get the fundamentals under your belt. If you're self-taught, go to the library and get lots of books. You can't lose by keeping a lot of books for reference. They're always great to lift your spirits and keep your level of quality up.

STORYBOARD

Ed Gombert was one of the new team at Disney who joined the studio in the early Seventies. Along with such talents as Don Bluth, Randy Cartwright, Glen Keane, John Lassiter and others, Gombert formed a crew that the studio hoped eventually would take over when the original "nine old men" retired. Gombert worked his way up to an animator, but the studio felt his visual sense and staging made him a better candidate for story. He's done story work on several films, including the Oscar-winning blockbuster The Little Mermaid.
We talked with Ed at his office in one of the many animation buildings Disney uses in Glendale. His walls were covered with sketches and ideas for the upcoming ALADDIN feature.

Ed Gombert

DATE: AUGUST 17, 1990

Q:
Could you just give a general description of your career.
A:
Okay. Well, I've worked for Disney almost exclusively from 1975. I came in through their animation training program and started out as an inbetweener on *The Rescuers*, the original feature. I moved up to animate on *Pete's Dragon*. At the end of *Pete's Dragon*, I was made a full animator and then animated on *Fox and the Hound*. After *Fox and Hound*, I spent a brief four months on *The Black Cauldron* and skipped over to *Mickey's Christmas Carol*, where I animated and did my first storyboarding under Burny Mattinson. Then I moved to *The Great Mouse Detective*, where I did sto-

ryboarding.
I Left Disney for a year to work on various Keebler cookie commercials and things like that. Then came back to Disney to work on the "Sport Goofy" project for a year. After that *The Great Mouse Detective* was still being made, (laughs) and I finished up animating on that. Next I moved over to Disney TV animation and did character design work on *Duck Tales* and some other shows that were never developed fully for production.
I came back to do storyboarding on *The Little Mermaid* and that was the first time I was officially classified as a story man and really got to learn the business of storyboarding. On *The Rescuers Down Under*, I did storyboarding again and stayed on to animate. That brings us up

60

to this year. I'm now doing work on the upcoming *Aladdin*.

Q:

What, if any, art training have you had?

A:

My original goal when I came out of high school was to go to Cal Arts. But Cal Arts hadn't opened up officially as a school when I graduated from high school. They were in a transition period and they weren't accepting any new students so I ended up going to a local junior college in Azusa, Citrus Community College. After two years of that I realized Cal Arts would be too expensive for my parents, so I went to Cal State Long Beach and put together my own program of classes that I thought would get me into animation.

Q:

How did you break into the business?

A:

The year I graduated from college, I submitted a portfolio to Hanna-Barbera and they turned me down. I was about to submit my portfolio to Filmation, but decided to mail it to Disney instead. I had been told there was no way you could get into Disney. There were no openings. Forget it. But, I decided what the heck, I'll send it anyway. It turned out Disney had an animation training program that nobody knew about and I got ac-

cepted. It was all very easy. (Laughs)

Q:
What does a storyboard artist do?

A:
Well. There's a system in animation, at least here at Disney, we refer to as "plussing". No matter what phase of the operation you're in, you're expected to make it better than it was when it came to your desk, whether you're animating or cleaning up the background or whatever.

In story, we take the script and we're supposed to visualize it, but more than that we're supposed to plus it, make it more entertaining. We bring the characters to life in "comic book" fashion. We have the freedom to explore relationships and come up with business that is more visually entertaining.

The way we storyboard here is different than any other studio. In other places where I've worked the director knows exactly what he wants and he dictates to the artists what he wants them to do. And on Saturday morning I know

the storyboard artists are, pretty much because of the lack of time, just visualizing the script. They pretty much do the layouts instead of what I consider storyboarding, which is fleshing out the personalities and exploring ideas. This is the only place in the world I know of that allows us the kind of freedom to explore situations and expand on the script. And that's why, if I couldn't storyboard here, I probably wouldn't be storyboarding. (Laughs)

Q:
At what point do you become involved with the project?
A:
Generally speaking, it's after the script has been written and a lot of visual exploratory work has been done. People have played around with character designs, played around with set designs, things like that. When I come on, I have a lot of information to draw from and I can focus on the characters' personalities and what they might be doing, while they're saying the lines that someone else has written.

Q:
How much assistance do you get from the writers and the directors?
A:
From the writers, that's tough, because in *Mermaid* and on *Aladdin* the directors are also the writers. It's not so much assistance as getting direction from the directors. In *The Rescuers Down Under*, I worked with them like anybody else around the department. You just work together trying to find the best ideas for the sequence, but generally speaking, when a writer has writ-

*A sequence from THE LITTLE MERMAID.
A: "What about the humans!"
B: "Humans?"
C: no dialogue
D: no dialogue
E: "Who said anything about humans?... heh, heh."
F: no dialogue*

ten a script, he goes away and that's that. The director is making his picture based on that script. Storyboarding follows the script just as layout follows storyboarding. They are separate aspects of production.

Q:

What is an average, daily routine for you as a storyboard artist?

A:

Well, if you're preparing for a presentation, your door is closed. You don't see anybody. You're sitting here cranking out ideas as fast as you can to present them to the directors, to get their okay, before it gets presented to Jeffrey Katzenberg or Peter Schneider.

Once it's presented to them, you get a list of their reactions and the directors decide how many of them they want to follow through on. That's what the average day is like. Once you've initially boarded a sequence there's months and months of corrections.

Q:

How much freedom are you given in this stage?

A:

In the very beginning, before there's a storyboard for each sequence, there's a lot of freedom. Because everybody is searching, even the directors, for the best ideas, the best things to happen, the best visuals. There's a lot of freedom at the beginning, but once there's a storyboard for each sequence, like I said, it's corrections after that and you're pretty much responding to other people's requests.

Q:

When do you finish with a project?

A:

I can be finished with a project when the next project is screaming for my help, or there's just nothing left to do. Depending on your status as a story person, you can be taken off early. The person that draws the best and has the best ideas could stay on for a long time. He updates sketches in the story reel to accommodate changes the producers want, or the directors want. That's a very boring part of the job and everybody hates being the last person off.

Q:

Do you think animation is a prerequisite for storyboarding?

A:

Definitely. As an animator you're combining the drawing and the acting. Storyboard people who don't have the animation experience, don't give as much information to the animators. It's

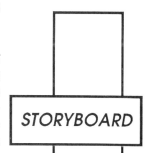

STORYBOARD

that idea of plussing, again. The more alive it looks on my board, the more character and fun I can put into the scenes, the more information the animator has to build on and improve, or plus, his animation. The animator has to work harder to pull the acting from a dull sketch than from a sketch that looks like, "Gee, all I have to do is inbetween that."

Q:

Speaking of adding a life to it, when you deal with a script is it harder to storyboard a bad script than a good script?

A:

Well, it depends on who's deciding it's a bad script. If the directors have decided it's a bad script, you have to figure out what it is they think is bad. If you think it's a bad script and they think it's a great script, (laughing) then you have the trouble of trying to figure out what they think is good about it!

That's probably the hardest part about storyboarding, picking the director's brain, trying to figure out what kind of movie he's trying to make. What he sees the character's personality as being. Once you find your boundaries of creativity, then you can go hog wild.

I think we have good script right now. It's not very specific. Everything hasn't been nailed down, just a lot of basic, good ideas, and good situations for characters. I would say a good script leaves me room to be creative.

A bad script would probably have a lot of detailed stuff that's pretty boring. Scripts that I hate have sections that are worded humorously. When you read it, it sounds very funny. When you take the words away and start thinking about what the situation is, you realize that there's very little there to storyboard. It's just a clever combination of words.

Q:

Personally, what project have you worked with that's given you the most personal satisfaction?

A:

Without a doubt, *The Little Mermaid* was the most satisfying. Because you could see the potential, when you read the script and it held on to that potential throughout the entire production. And a lot of what I did, as a storyboard artist, stayed in the film (laughing) and was animated.

One of the saddest things about storyboarding is how many changes it can undergo once you're finished with it. The layout man can change the staging. Or the animator may come up with another way of doing it, and your idea is gone and now it's someone else's idea. That's the down side of plussing. In *Little Mermaid,* a lot of what I did stayed in the film. That's the most gratifying part, to sit down and watch the "Under the Sea" sequence and just see my storyboards brought to life by the animators. That's when storyboarding is the most fun.

Q:

So that was a sequence you were key in.

A:

Right. That's about 90 percent of what I boarded. That and the sequence that follows it where Sebastian spills the beans. That was challenging. The song was easy for the most part because I had the timing and pacing of the sequence. And when they say things like "the carp plays the harp," there's not too many things you can do except a carp playing a harp.

But in the following sequence, we just have dialogue between the king and the crab. You have to punch it up to make it more interesting by coming up with visual ideas that are entertaining. Such as Sebastian crying into the king's beard, or having all his knees knocking together, when he's really nervous. That's the most challenging part, taking a script that's just talking heads, and trying to come up with visually entertaining ideas.

Q:
What would you say was a failed project that you worked on, that may have been commercially successful?
A:

I thought about this one and it may be wrong of me to say it, because I never saw the finished film, but to me *The Black Cauldron* was the biggest miss. Half way through production I knew it couldn't live up to what we saw in Mel Shaw's sketches in 1975. That film was a low point in many people's careers (laughing) at the studio. They went with every typical, unimaginative solution to telling the story they could think of. Everyone wanted to make *The Black Cauldron* , but not the one the studio made.

Q:
If you were to start today to think about being a storyboard artist, what would you feel you would need to know, or do?
A:

Acting. That's the main thing. When I was going to school, I thought the key to being a Disney artist was the ability to draw well. I focused all my attention on drawing classes and I learned, once I got here, how important acting is to the whole thing. I have since taken some acting classes and feel certain that it's a valuable experience for all areas of animation. Acting is so crucial for the animator and you don't always see it in a storyboard. That's one of the reasons I am storyboarding today.

In *Fox and Hound* there was a sequence of Big Mama and Vixie talking; just shots of heads back and forth. I said, "This is boring. Nobody comes to an animated film to listen to characters talk." I did some thumbnails of what I would have the characters doing and the directors liked it. During the production of *Mickey's Christmas Carol*, the director, Burny Mattinson, liked my ideas and suggestions so much he asked me to board the section where Willie the Giant takes scrooge to see Mickey's family. After that I knew storyboarding was what I wanted to do.

STORYBOARD

Mitch Schauer

DATE: JULY 26, 1990

Q:
Please give a brief description of your career, including the studios you've worked for and specific productions you've worked on.

A:
Actually my schooling and my career kind of overlapped each other. I started right out of high school actually in a graphics arts studio in Tulsa and designed cartoons and labels and all that kind of crap you do. They saw that I had a knack for cartooning so I did a lot of that and was involved in a lot of print art, print work, that kind of thing. While I was there I found out about Cal Arts, so I sent my portfolio there and they asked me to come out. So, I started at Cal Arts and went there for almost a year and realized I didn't want to just know cartooning so I left there. I then went down to Art Center and got my degree in advertising administration.

While I was at Art Center during summer school, a girl told me about a job opening at Filmation so I went over and applied. I interviewed with Don Christianson and Herb Hazleton and they were asking me all kinds of questions like, "you know all about bike pans and about field guides?" And I said, "oh, yeah!" I had a buddy down in the lobby and they gave us a break, they wanted me to go draw a Flash Gordon scene for the feature and see if I could do it or not. So, I ran down to the lobby and asked my buddy to go to the ink and paint department and ask what a bike pan was and about field guides.

BOBBY'S WORLD SIZE COMPARISON

WEBBLY   UNCLE TED   DAD   BOBBY   MOM   ROGER   KELLY   DEREK

So, by the time I got my job I had the field guides and I knew what a bike pan was. I started out in layout with Filmation. After about a year of that, they moved me up to storyboard just because they couldn't find someone. They were looking for a support artist and I said I can do it so they put me there. From Filmation, they laid me off and I finished Art Center and went to Disney and worked in publicity under Bill Moore for about a year and worked on *Fox and the Hound* and that kind of thing doing posters and mark-ups for posters and storyboards for trailers and that kind of thing.

I left Disney after a year because there was too much politics. it was under that Ron Miller regime and I wasn't happy there. So I packed up the family and went back to Tulsa and went to work for an ad agency. I worked in the ad agency for two years. They made me head of their multi-image department and we made big slide shows for all kinds of things. Again, I worked in print, designing ads, speccing type, all the kind of things that go along with advertising, which was good for me. I think advertising teaches you how to be versatile because you'll do an ad for an oil company and the next ad you do is for a pizza company and I felt that was a big help to me.

After two years of that and still freelancing back here for Hanna-Barbera doing storyboards, I decided that if I didn't get back out here and get back into business, that I was doomed. So, I packed up the

The cast of BOBBY'S WORLD

© Film Roman

family and came back and went to work for Hanna-Barbera as associate producer under Kay Wright and was associate producer on *Pink Panther and Sons* and the *Gobot* series. Then Jean MacCurdy asked me if I wanted to produce Scooby Doo so I took that and I produced a season of that and the *Star Fairies* special and the *Pound Puppies* special.

I then got a job offer from Marvel to come over and do *Inhumanoids* and the *G.I. Joe* feature. But I just stayed for the *Inhumanoids* and part of the *Blondie* special. I got frustrated with that. At that time the fellow who brought the Smurfs over here from Belgium was starting up a company and asked me if I'd like to come over and be Director of Creative Development for it.

So, I went over there for almost two years and we developed shows and all kinds of characters. I think the first year I was there we developed 27 shows, all kinds, action adventure and all that kind of thing. At the end of that, they were kind of slowing down so I left there and got a call from Scott Jeralds saying George Singer needed someone at Film Roman to take Brett Koth's place so I came over here and I've been here; it will be two-and-a-half years this September. That's where I be.

Q:
What does a character designer do?
A:
What you hope you do is you get a feel for the show and you get a feel for the client, what they're trying to convey, the feeling of the show and the type of humor or the type of action. Then you try to design a character that fits into their mind set. You try different types of characters, different styles and the client or the studio picks the one that they like the best and you're on your way.

Q:
Can you give me at least one good and one bad example of what you consider in the area of character design?
A:
I think a good example would be Jay Ward and the Bullwinkle characters and Dudley Do-Right characters because they were designed for a budget and simplicity. They looked funny and I think that's a key to a funny show is that the character should look funny even if they're not moving or they're not saying anything. A good example for a live action adventure type of show obviously to me is *Jonny Quest*. Doug Wildey, being so involved in that, and them bringing out all the comic book artists to work along behind the animators and the designers, because those characters were designed very simply for animation. That's tough to do: action adventure and keep them simple. And Alex Toth was a good example of how to do it on a budget. So, a lot of times I think that the money determines what the characters look like, how involved they are. But, those are good examples.

Bad example, I think that a bad character is one that when it's designed doesn't have a construction sense to it and you can't turn it around. A lot of the toy shows that I've worked on are bad examples of having to take a toy and redesign it for animation when they're not made for it. There are a lot of those, take your pick.

BOBBY'S WORLD ®

SHOW NO. 6412

SCENE NO.

MODEL

BOBBY G.

KELLY

DEREK

ROGER

The cast of BOBBY'S WORLD as they appear in a Peanuts satire for the "Bobby's Big Broadcast" episode of BOBBY'S WORLD.

© Film Roman

Q:
When do you get involved in a show?
A:
That's a tough question. Well, for instance on the Bobby show we designed those characters before we even pitched the show. Then we got together with the writers and Howie [Mandell] and they liked the designs and we just followed through with those.

When you get into a show, once it's in series, usually the designer gets the script, right after it's been approved, obviously. Then they go through and they make a whole list of the characters and the props and that kind of thing and they start designing hopefully before the board artist starts, so the board artist has reference. Sometimes I've seen boards done, especially here at

CHARACTER DESIGN

the studio, before we've had the models done, and did the models based on the storyboard. So, it kind of depends on the schedule.

Q:

How do you go about designing an original character for animation?

A:

To me, I think if you're going to do a funny character it helps to go down and talk to the guys [at the studio] a lot, and get a feel. Just hear something funny or talk about something funny. That will kick me off a lot of times. Sometimes I will look at a storyboard from another show and see a doodle in there that looks pretty funny and that will get me going. Sometimes it's just the attitude of the character. If it's an angry character you try to accent the eyebrows and the mouth to make him look angry. So, you just try to push it and all the facial features, you try to push them in areas to accent a particular personality or attitude. That's where I usually start.

Q:

How different is that from adapting a character from another medium?

A:

Obviously you have to retain the integrity and the look of that character, so that's a little more limited. As an example, working on the *Pound Puppies*, we had these ugly dolls and we had to do ugly drawings. But, you had to put as much personality into those clumps of whatever those things were. You had to put personality into those so we tried to do as much as we could, and it's usually in the eyes and the mouth and the body posing. So, you try to pick up on the most unique as-

pects of the character and see if you can push those along further and keep them in character but still try to get them more into an animated arena.

Q:

In your current position, where you both design characters and oversee those who design characters, what is an average daily routine?

A:

If you're going to design characters, I like to start off with a script. I spend a lot of time, not so much reading the script, I read the script very quickly and then I spend a lot of time just thinking about it and, again, talking to people and walking around, that kind of thing. You try to get as many ideas into your head as you can and then sit down. For me it works. I sit down at the last minute and I can do them as fast as I possibly can because all the ideas are in my head, I've been thinking about them so long. So, it's not a normal routine for you to sit down and you start drawing in the morning. It's not regimented as much as I guess some artists are.

Q:

How much freedom are you given on an average production?

A:

As far as character design, once you've established the main cast, you don't have much freedom as far as what you can do with those characters. On Garfield you had a specific look to a character, so the only creative freedom you really had might be in costuming or in an extreme action when we had Garfield in the G force as in *Invasion of the Giant Robots* where he was pressed in a chair and we had him spread over the edge of the chair. Sometimes you can do that. I think a lot more of the creativity comes out of the incidental characters. As long as they retain the style, as in Garfield. One of the key things to Garfield are the big eyes. So, if you retain the look of the show so people say that the character belongs in a Garfield show, then you can do just about anything you want. That's why I enjoy the secondary characters a lot.

Q:

What project or production have you done that has given you the most professional enjoyment, and why?

A:

Probably *Bobby's World* because (of) not only being the designer of the characters initially, but also being the producer on it. *Bobby's World* is the first time that I've had control with regard to working with the writers and the story editor to where the designs, as far as I felt, made a difference that I wanted to do. So, that's been the joy of *Bobby's World* is making it look the way I want it to look, whereas in the past, producing shows for other studios, you were handed a show and that's what it was.

Q:

What, in your opinion, on the opposite spectrum, would be a failed project that you personally felt disappointed with, or with the final outcome?

A:

I'd have to say *The Gobots* because when I designed the characters for the Gobots, obviously they were toys first. But, what I tried to do is take those little toys, those little figures and make them more of an animated char-

acter (different from) transformers, which were very blocky and very mechanical looking. I tried to give the Gobots more personality and simplify them and I think that it was the initial show, the five-part miniseries, it was just hurt because of the time crunch. We went into production on that in June and had to deliver I believe it was September. It wasn't overseas very long. So, I think that was the biggest disappointment because we had high hopes for that being a fun action adventure type show.

Q:

Finally, if you were to start in the business today, or if you were to give someone advice to get into the business, what would it be?

A:

I'm glad I went to Art Center and got a degree in something other than cartooning because I think versatility is the key thing to being in the cartoon business. And, if you are versatile, you can go to work in the studio and they don't pigeonhole you. One day you can be drawing cartoon characters and the next day they can put you on a Jonny Quest-type show and you can do it. So, if anybody's getting into the business, I would advise them to learn to draw. That's one thing I learned in Art Center is having instructors saying the kids that come to the school today, they don't know how to draw. A lot of the art schools don't teach drawing as strongly as they used to. I think that's the key to anything, any aspect of animation is you've got to know how to draw.

CHARACTER DESIGN

Mike Giaimo's distinctive designs have kept him busy at studios since he left school. Whether at Disney, Warner Brothers or freelancing, Mike keeps continually active. As well as working on numerous films, he regularly teaches future designers at Cal Arts.
We interviewed Mike at the Warners Classic Animation offices. His desk is surrounded by vivid color drawings of locations and humorous character designs, as well as a number of small plastic figures of classic animated characters.

Mike Giaimo

DATE: JULY 23, 1990

Q:
Could you please give a brief description of your career, including studios you've worked for and specific productions you've worked on.

A:
I started right out of school at Disney in June of 1978. That was my first professional job. They were doing production on *The Fox and the Hound* at the time. I was a trainee and I went from trainee to inbetweener on *Fox and Hound* and got up to assistant animation working under John Musker. After my first few weeks of assisting I don't know (laughing) if they didn't like my animation or what but at any rate, a couple of people, I think it was mostly Glen Keane and Randy Cartwright, saw that I had some

potential for development and story.

At that time they were starting story development on *The Black Cauldron*. I was put into story development on *Cauldron* with Pete Young, a very gifted storyman. I was on *Cauldron* for only eight months. After that I worked with Darrell van Citters on a little short called *Fun with Mr. Future* doing character and story design. After the short, a property was dropped off to Tom Wilhite's office. It was the galley proofs of *Who Censored Roger Rabbit* and they put Darrell and I on it initially. Believe it or not, I was on that for two years doing initial production design and lots of character designs from 1981 to 1982.

After *Roger Rabbit* , which went nowhere during the Ron

72

Miller period, I was put on various projects developing Mickey Mouse featurettes. *Mickey Columbus* was one, I remember. I did some work for Tokyo Disneyland developing some animation that was used in conjunction with audio animatronic figures for one of their pavilions there. I also did some design work for Epcot's seas' pavilion. I was on *Great Mouse Detective* for two weeks. Basically my career was one where I would usually dodge features (laughs), you might say.

I've never been known as a feature person. Usually my taste is a little more eclectic; a little more offbeat. So after a period of short term projects, which may have been about two and a half to three years, they put me back on *Roger Rabbit* when Ron Miller left and Spielberg took over with Zemeckis slated as director. For a brief period Darrell and I were on it and they had me redesign Roger, toning him down, with Zemeckis' suggestion to "make him a little more like Michael J. Fox," because my Roger was a bit too clown-like (laughs).

I started freelancing in 1986, working for small production houses as well as Hanna-Barbera, Southern Star Productions, Kroyer Films and Hyperion Films, where I did character designs for *The Brave Little Toaster*. My freelance stint lasted for three-and-a-half years until 1989, when I went to work for Warner Brothers in Classic Animation as a production designer.

Q:
What schooling, if any, did you have in animation?

A:

My first real training was at Cal Arts. I had a couple years at a junior college, where I took some art classes and a brief stint at Hot Dog On A Stick, but it was really Cal Arts that gave me real insight into animation and film making. At the end of my second year at Cal Arts, Disney saw the work I had done there and asked me to work for them.

Q:

As you do both layout and production design, can you explain both tasks?

A:

A layout artist is one who actually sets the stage for the animation. He will design a sequence, shot by shot, breaking it down scenically and cinematically, working closely with the director, who has a great degree of control as to the shots themselves. So the layout artist designs the environmental stage in which the characters are going to be placed.

A production designer or an art director, which is what I do at this moment, is a little different from a layout artist. A layout artist will follow an art director, who sets the whole style of a picture and the aesthetic tone of what it's going to be. And an art director will often incorporate, which a layout artist usually doesn't do, color sketches that will be followed later on by a background artist or reinterpreted by a background artist to help set what kind of approach the color is going to take as well. So I will set up not only the graphic but also the color sensibility of a production.

Q:

Would you say this would be closer to what the layout man back in what they call the classic days of shorts did?

A:

Yes, I would say so.

Q:

As opposed to TV?

A:

Right. Television is so much more compartmentalized that it has to be broken down more stringently to adhere to time schedules and air dates.

Q:

Speaking of design layouts and production design, can you give me an example of good and bad work that a person could look at.

A:

I think *101 Dalmatians* is a great example of wonderful layout. When I speak of layout, again I will mix layout and art direction together because I think they are intertwined. Some people will say layout and they'll think "oh, a person who really knows perspective; a person who can stage and render the heck out of anything." I think those are, indeed, certain qualifications but I think over and above that what really sets a great layout artist and/or art director apart from the rest is someone who has an individual POV [point of view] that he or she can offer to a particular film that will always enhance, never detract from the character because it's always the character that is the thing. I prefer films that have very, very strong art direction styles and are extremely design oriented.

Getting back to *101 Dalmatians*, it has a spirit and a wit that is reflected in the story and the characters that I think is just beautiful. Everything is meshed together so well in that film. *Sleeping Beauty* is another choice; not so great on story, but an art director's dream! There's a totally unique yet believable world that Eyvind Earle created for that film - very lyrical and consistent throughout.

I also think a film such as *Alice in Wonderland* is a beautiful example of great art direction. When you look at the layouts, even though they are very caricatured and stylized, you'll find an extreme amount of control and restraint. In fact, a lot of the layouts are vignetted. In other words, there are dark areas around the sides and just a spotlight effect on the character or on a group situation. It's one of the darkest films, literally, that Disney ever did.

Pinocchio is dark in total mood but *Alice* is actually the darkest film in terms of color and styling. For being such a wild film with such eccentric characters, its mood with this vignette style creates a focus and a nice balance for all the eccentricity that takes place, so I really respond to that film in the way that it balances out. In blending layout with color and design, it's one of the most readable films, because you'll notice that the background values are very, very dark so that the characters become luminous and stand out. Almost in every scene you'll see that the characters pop forward where the backgrounds, as ec-

centric as some of them are, tend to recede. I respond to that film very, very much.

I would also have to include Maurice Noble's work at Warner Brothers. His Ralph Phillips' se-

ries and *Duck Dodgers* are, I think, stellar examples of what you can do with creative design and color and layout, without a Disney budget.

A great production designer will take you somewhere that is familiar and yet unfamiliar. It's like the plausible impossible. You believe it and yet it's just different enough. He'll take you on a fantastic journey but have you rooted enough so that you're not lost or alienated. Take *Song of the South,* for instance. You wouldn't think of this film as the most intriguing, art direction-wise, but I think it's wonderful. The "Zippety-Do-Dah" sequence calls to mind a beautiful spring day that you've experienced, but yet the color and the design takes it over the top. It elevates it so that it's even *grander* and more whimsical than the most beautiful spring day you've ever experienced. That's successful art direction; the power to communicate mood and feeling to an audience in a unique and intriguing way.

BEACH BLANKET BUGS

© Warner Bros.

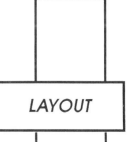

LAYOUT

In *101 Dalmatians* , even though it took place within a contemporary time frame, the design of the furniture, interiors and exteriors had a sense of caricature, a sense of whimsy, a sense of fun and uniqueness. If you're going to render and do things exactly as they are, why even bother doing it? Take people somewhere they haven't been before.

In my opinion, an example of a weaker film in terms of good layout/art direction would be *The Aristocrats*. I thought the contemporary styling inappropriate, failing to capture the mood and atmosphere of a Parisian town at the turn of the century. In other words, it seemed to rely on some past Disney efforts and was, at best, a mediocre solution.

Q:

When do you generally get involved with a project?

A:

I prefer to get involved from the very beginning. I've experienced situations where I have accepted a project, but have come in on the middle. (Laughs) As a production designer, I have to be involved right from the beginning, even if the boards are in a state of flux or only a rough treatment is available. I work best with a blank sheet of paper. If a film has already been set stylistically it's too late for me.

Q:

How much assistance do you get from the director and the storyboard people?

A:

Actually I get a lot of assistance. We all need help in this business (laughs). I work very, very closely with the director. He will definitely guide me in certain areas. I think we all need to

be pushed and the director often provides that extra nudge that will send you over the top.

The story people may have an idea and if it requires a certain scenic set that needs to be designed, I'll come up with visual ideas and concepts. I feel very fortunate coming from an animation and story background, so whenever I do production designing I never think the layout is the thing. I'm constantly thinking of how to best support the character. I try to be sensitive to the overall concept.

Q:

Do you have a particularly strong area in your layout or design field?

A:

I would say my strongest suit would be my sense of design, color and style. I'm not a production designer that people hire to be a chameleon. I'm best with my particular point of view.

Q:

What is a daily routine for you?

A:

I probably start out doing some rough production designing, which could incorporate some color sketches, as well as pencil drawings, and working with the background artist on any given production, overseeing the color sensibility. I'll also confer with the director in terms of the storyboarding process and how I can best aid in that.

Q:

Is most of your day spent at the drawing board or are you more coordinating?

A:

I would say at least 70 percent is spent at the board. The rest would be coordinating.

Q:

How much freedom are you given on each production?

A:

I'm given, by and large, a great amount of freedom because people who would hire me to do a job would know what they're getting up front (laughs).

Q:

What project have you been associated with that's given you the most professional enjoyment and satisfaction? Whether the project was a success or not is not important.

A:

I would say there were two; my development work on *Roger Rabbit* , as a designer, and my art direction at Warner Brothers Classic Animation starting with *Box Office Bunny*. Only because those tend to be the two that made me grow and stretch the most. I am having a great time and I always try to have a good time at whatever I do, but the projects that tend to be the most personally satisfying are the ones that usually (chuckles) cause the most pain.

Q:

Which would you consider would be a failed project, one that you weren't satisfied with?

A:

I could say *Roger* . I could say *The Black Cauldron*, (chuckles) that's an easy one. I suppose it would be *Roger Rabbit* . I really admire the technical dexterity and the incredible visual style of it [the final film]. Since I do come from a story background, though, I felt that from a character standpoint, just from a personality standpoint of character

animation it fell short, but it certainly had enough visual appeal to keep people amused.

Q:

If you were to start in the business today or if you were to give someone advice for starting the business how would you have them prepare?

A:

Art direction requires the culling of so many experiences in animation; to get a sensibility of what the story is, what character motivation is, so that the whole scenic backdrop can play to that. It requires an understanding of basic drawing skills, and staging, but more than that, a keen sense of aesthetics and a real sensitivity towards art and art history to bring the production styling to a working whole

The entire process of animation and I would venture to think that as an art director the only one who would even have a bigger grasp of that would be a director, who even sees the whole picture. I oversee it graphically, but that isn't to say that other art directors should have a strong background and all of that, but I know that just for setting the stage for the characters it has really come in handy, knowing the entire process and having been involved in it.

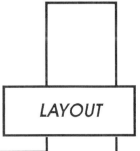

LAYOUT

Bob Givens is one of the grand masters of animation still highly active in the business. Though his career began at the Disney studio, he quickly moved over to Warner's, where he handled a large number of chores from character design (such as the first model sheet of Bugs Bunny), to layout to storyboard. A selection of his model sheets, for such characters as Bugs, Elmer and Little Hiawatha, appear in Steve Schneider's *That's All Folks: The Art of Warner Bros. Animation*. After Warner's, he moved on to a number of other studios, returning to Warner's in the Seventies to work on several of the compilation features.

We found Givens at his desk at Film Roman, where he currently is doing key layouts for *Zazoo U. The series debuted in the Fall of 1990 on Fox Saturday morning schedule.*

Bob Givens

DATE: AUGUST 16, 1990

Q:

Could you please give a brief description of your career, including studios you've worked for, and the productions you've worked on?

A:

Well, I started at Disney in 1937. They were hiring for *Snow White* and I started out in animation checking. We had to [at Disney] and it was great training. We didn't check too long because we were waiting to go on a film, but at least we had about three or four months of it. We learned camera and the whole bit. Everybody should do it when they start out.

I worked mostly on the duck as part of the Donald Duck wing. From Disney's I went over to Schlesinger's studio to work with Chuck Jones and Friz [Freleng] and Tex [Avery] and those guys. At Warner's I did the boards for maybe 500 pictures, the classics. I worked with [writers] Mike Maltese and Warren Foster and the bunch. They would usually write and make some little kind of scribble. I'd put it in more comprehensive form. The boards were pretty close to the finished product, at least in the expressions. Mel Blanc recorded from those damn things! They were looser but it was all there. At the same time I was doing boards, I was also doing characters. I'd spend a couple of weeks on the board, then whatever time was needed on characters.

Then from there I went over to UPA. In the Fifties I did 10 years of nothing but commercials and

Layout from an episode of GARFIELD AND FRIENDS.

© Film Roman

industrial films. I even did the first Raid bug commercials. Hal Mason and I did the work. I did the board in 1953 and we did it on spec. We sent it to the agency and figured that's the end of it. They loved it and we did them for 17 years. I boarded them, laid them out, painted the backgrounds, did everything but animate them. Tex [Avery] came in on the last batch done in color.

I then worked at Hanna-Barbera and a little bit of every place in town. I guess that about covers it up to now.

Q:
What actual art schooling did you have, if any?
A:
Lots of it. I went to Chouinard, mostly nights, and then I went to Bistram School, New York Art Students League and Jepson School in Los Angeles. Quite a bit of art training there and over the years.

Q:
Why and how did you break into this business?
A:
Well, I knew a guy, Hardie Gramatky, who worked at Disney's, when I was in high school. He got me in there, he and Don Graham. They thought I had potential, so they greased the pole for me (laughing). The first film I worked on was *The Old Mill*. I started as a checker on that and then I went into production on *Snow White*.

Q:
What does a layout artist do?
A:

79

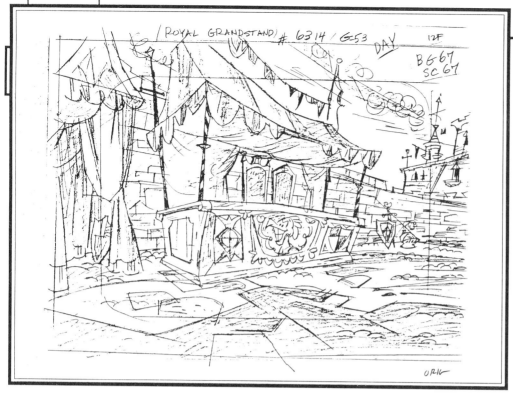

things [UPA for TV]. They were okay but there weren't any stories. There was nothing much to work with. If I was doing a bad layout it was because of a bad story and too much of a rush.

Q:
What would make a bad layout?
A:
The layout just doesn't function, or the cuts are bad. There's no or inadequate hook-ups to other scenes and no motivations. Things just happen for no reason. That's a bad layout.

Q:
When does a layout artist usually get involved with the project?
A:
Usually after the board is done. He takes over from that.

Q:
How much assistance do you get from the director or the storyboard artist?
A:
Well, quite a lot on good boards. Even if they're not good boards, you have to make 'em work anyway. But it's usually enough to jump off on if the board guys are competent enough to tell the story. You can take lib-

Well, he plans the whole thing. Whether it's a sequence or a commercial, or whatever it is, he plans it. He sets up the characters in their positions. He designs the sets and the background. He also works out the mechanics somewhat, such as the pan lengths. He kind of analyzes what's to be done and then picks a simple way to do it. That's what I'd say. He just plans the picture before the director gets to it.

Q:
Can you name some films that you think have good or bad layouts?
A:
Oh, yeah. At Warners, the old *Termite Terrace*, they had good layouts. And then the UPA *Magoos* were great.

Q:
Can you think of some film that might have what you consider poor layouts?
A:
Well, yeah. The *Popeye* stuff we did in the Sixties [for King features] and the *Magoo/Tracy*

erties within that story, but basically it's all there. Then it's just a matter of shifting elements a little here and there so that they'll work in animation.

Q:

As a layout person, where do you think your strengths are in the layout?

A:

I think in just setting up simple scenes that save a lot of money. You know, getting the effect without doing the work. Like camera mechanics, if you can accomplish the effect without getting heavily involved in the mechanics you save the production a lot of time. I can simplify the mechanics. I'm also good at drawing.

Q:

Does the layout artist need to know mechanics?

A:

Oh, yeah. Well, he can get by without it but I don't know how. You almost have to think mechanics, like pans, the speeds, hook-ups (how to get from one thing to another), etc. And how to have things hook up, even if it's way down the line in the picture.

Q:

In an average day, what do you do?

A:

Well, I do maybe four or five scenes. I do the backgrounds and the characters and some kind of notes on color or this and that. It's just to pin down the scene for the animator. He takes that character drawing and all he's got to do is just touch it up a little. He's got it made!

I try to play up the characters, the animation. Keep it in the

clear, that's my word. Because the name of the game is animation. Backgrounds should hold their place and enhance the animation. Avoid things like tangents and dark on dark and light on light.

Q:

Do you ever use reference?

A:

Well, yeah, I do. I go to the library and I try to research the scene. Even if it's a design of some goofy looking thing, it's still got to be based on some kind of reality. Sometimes I'll invent the whole thing, but most of the time I will get some research or remember something I've done in the past.

Q:

How are realistic layouts different than broader, cartoony layouts?

A:

They're harder. That, and they never look right for some reason. It's just too close to live action. No matter how well drawn it is, it just doesn't look right. In a cartoon you can get away with murder, because it's imagination. Realistic ones are the hardest things I ever did and I did a lot of those real things at Hanna-Barbera and Filmation. They never look right. They look like puppets. They look like they're frozen. It's just something in the translation.

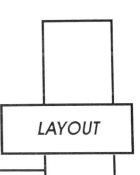

LAYOUT

Q:

How much freedom are you given on average productions?

A:

Well, as much as you want, as long as it doesn't go too crazy and as long as it tells the story. You can re-stage a little here and there to make it better. And that's where we have flexibility. But you can't depart too far from the boards because that's what everyone else refers to. If it's too far off, they're going to say, "what is it?" And I've seen it happen with some!

Q:

How would you say doing layouts for the shorts, or Disney features differs from television?

A:

Well, you had more time to pin them down back then, especially on the features. And also, you worked over all of them, rather than in TV where you do a section here, and a section there. Doing the whole thing is a lot easier to do. With UPA we took even longer because they were so designed. It makes a big difference, that few days here and there.

Q:

Do you enjoy working with more designed boards?

A:

Well, it's all different. I like them all. I've done everything from straight shows to wild and crazy Bullwinkle. It's all drawing, just different kinds.

Q:

What project or work has given you the most professional satisfaction?

A:

Well, there were a bunch of them. I mean different things.

Like for instance the early *Termite Terrace*, the UPAs, and the Fifties where I did nothing but commercials and industrial films. We did a thing for NASA, which raised the money for the eventual moon trip. I worked with Frank Capra for a year. We designed capsules, the suits, the whole bit, from imagination. Then NASA and the engineers built it.

Q:

What have you worked on that you thought was a failed project?

A:

Well, one of the biggest I can think of off hand were those so-called features we did where we used old stuff and new stuff. They were nothing but bridges between old cartoons. You can't do it because the characters were bigger in the old days and then you suddenly got a different, more recent short and had to try to hook those things up. It was murder, and it looks it. It was just a patch job. The stories were okay, but it was just the look and that continuity.

Q:

If you were to start today doing layouts, what sort of training would you suggest?

A:

Well, if a kid hasn't been to school, I'd say go to school. Go to a place like Cal Arts or Otis or USC or UCLA, somewhere that stresses drawing and design. Drawing is the basis of all this business. You can't get too much of it.

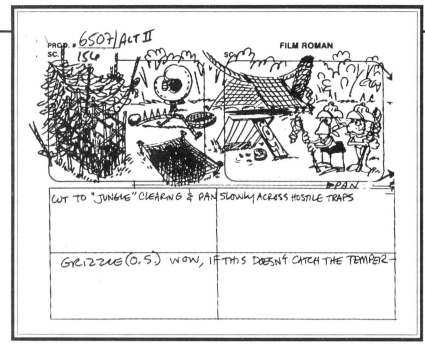

Left: Storyboard panel from ZAZOO U
Below: The layout created from it

© Film Roman

LAYOUT

Bill Lorencz

DATE: JULY 27, 1990

Q:
Could you please give a brief description of your career, including studios you've worked for and specific productions you've worked on?

A:
Okay, I started out in high school. I worked for Western Publishing Company doing children's books and games, puzzles, things like that with animation characters. I went from that to Hanna-Barbera doing TV animation backgrounds and subsequently, other studios, all in animation. Filmation, briefly, Ruby-Spears, advertising animation, Film Fair and some of those places that do commercial TV advertisements. Then, Don Bluth's, Bagdasarian Productions, Chipmunk Productions and Disney, working for TV animation, basically painting backgrounds and initially starting out painting production backgrounds for the animation studios. Gradually, as you gain experience, you go into keying, which is basically what I'm doing now, background keying. I don't actually paint animation backgrounds now. I'm painting keys that other painters will be using to paint the production backgrounds.

Q:
What are some of the actual productions you worked on?

A:
Going back into Hanna-Barbera days, *Herculoids* and *Jonny Quest* and any number of those. I just worked from one production to another. Then there

84

were theatricals, *The Secret of Nimh* and *American Tail, the Chipmunks' Adventure*. At Disney, I've worked on *Chip and Dale's Rescue Rangers* and *Duck Tales*, a brief encounter with *Duck Tales*, but mostly *Rescue Rangers* and *Tail Spin*. Hopefully more.

Q:

What schooling did you have?

A:

None, basically. I was in junior high school and I went to an art class and there was a fellow that was teaching the art class who worked for Western Publishing Company. He thought I had talent and said I could apprentice with him. So I started during my senior year, I went four-four, part day school and part day at his studio, and before I graduated high school, I was getting books and games published. So when I graduated high school, I was already working and it was just a flow from there.

Q:

How did you get into the animation field?

A:

The fellow that I had worked with and I had come up with a puppet of Huckleberry Hound. That was in the beginning when Joe Barbera had just started. We took it over to Joe Barbera and he said that he couldn't do anything with it because he had licensed the character out; we'd have to see Knickerbocker Toys. Knickerbocker Toys looked and said it's too expensive to put out. Joe said, "Well, forget the puppet, I want you to work for me."

SPACE ACE, the vido game

So, I started working with Hanna-Barbera. Then, once I'd worked there, wherever I went I had a reference in the business.

Q:

What does a background key artist do?

A:

A background key artist gets a layout and he has to establish the mood and the atmosphere of the stage that the characters are going to play on. So, he takes a line drawing that a layout man has done or maybe he's done himself and talks with the director to establish what kind of a mood they want to get involved with. Is it a night shot? Is it a dark, sinister shot? Is it a happy, day shot? Then you have to go through reference material or just out of your head. When you've done it long enough, you can just fabricate the coloring and lighting you want, to establish and create the stage that the characters are going to play on.

Q:

What are the tools you generally work with?

A:

Basically, I try to use Liquitex brushes. The red sable brushes seem to be the most efficient for the keys that we're using. We use round series brushes with the sharp point. I use flat, chiseled brushes for broad areas. I use Badger brushes for smoothing areas out, blending areas. Airbrush is an important tool basically for keeping the board wet and for tinting areas, more so than working with friskets and things like that. Paints: I use Cel Vinyl which is an industry product. Well, it can be purchased now outside in some art stores. Cartoon Color is selling them.

Gouache, acrylic, or any one of those mediums may be applicable to this job.

Q:

How do you personally go about converting a layout into a background?

A:

First of all, you have to trace it down onto a board. I happen to use Strathmore, series 500, regular surface, cold press. That's not an advertisement. It's a very nice surface to work on. It's almost like a nice watercolor paper, only it's got this firm board texture. I trace it down with graphite paper and then proceed by starting with a wash underpainting and then building up to a more opaque surface. I try to control surfaces with textures and things like that to make it interesting so it isn't all one, even look. Basically, that's how it's done.

Sometimes, if you don't have a picture in your mind of what you want to do, you get magazines or go to a reference library. If you're doing an interior of a castle or something and you just can't really visualize what that would look like, look for reference on castles and get a visual picture. As opposed to directly translating that picture that you're looking at onto what you're doing, you just get the flavor of it, the colors, and the values and then you apply it to what you're doing.

Q:

Who do you generally work with, besides background artists, on a production?

A:

Well, basically, you work with your director, number one, because he's telling you what he wants to see on the screen. But on more of a craftsman level, you work with the color key artist, who's going to do the color keying for the characters, because it's important that the background and their characters meld together so the characters read well on screen. And then you work, quite often with the layout artists themselves, determining what the important areas are and then defining some of their line work in how they want it to be interpreted. So, it's a cooperative effort. The more cooperative you are, the more successful you are in an overall product.

Q:
Could you give me an example of a film that you would consider to be a film with good backgrounds and a film with bad backgrounds? How would someone discern that by looking?

A:

Well, obviously, *The Secret of Nimh* was a beautiful film. Any of the early Disney films were beautiful films: *Bambi*'s softness, the ethereal feelings that were in *Fantasia*, beautiful background work. The early Disney films almost to the film were excellent and have not been attainable since. But in the current films being done, *The Secret of Nimh* was beautiful background-wise. *American Tail* had scenes that were really beautifully done.

As far as failure goes, in backgrounds, Filmation's *Pinocchio and the Emperor of the Night* might be considered an appropriate example. I don't know whether it's a matter of time, or whether it's lack of people understanding the feature look, they're just not very nicely painted.

Q:
Are there more specific reasons other than they're just not well painted?

A:

Just the control of surfaces, the colors, the attention to detail, the atmosphere or lack thereof that's created. If you don't have a specific ambience about a room, you end up with flat walls with hard shadows on them,. That, to me, is unattractive unless you're doing Daffy Duck or something of that genre. Then that is handsome for that type of cartoon. But as far as feature animation, even *Oliver* had some very poor painting, but it also had some very rich painting. In feature productions, the painting quality varies with the individual. There were some absolutely beautiful paintings in *Mermaid* but there were some places that just made me grit my teeth.

Puzzle from
THE SECRET
OF NIMH

© Mrs. Brisby
Ltd.

BACKGROUND

With the time schedule, one person or one particular person who is maybe better than another person can't do the whole show. So you have this imbalance in backgrounds. Almost every film has it, even the old Disney films.

A:
It's pretty much come in in the morning and get your supplies out and lay your palette out, get your water and your brushes together, and start painting. Paint until the end of the day.

Back cover to THE SECRET OF NIMH paint book

© Western Publishing

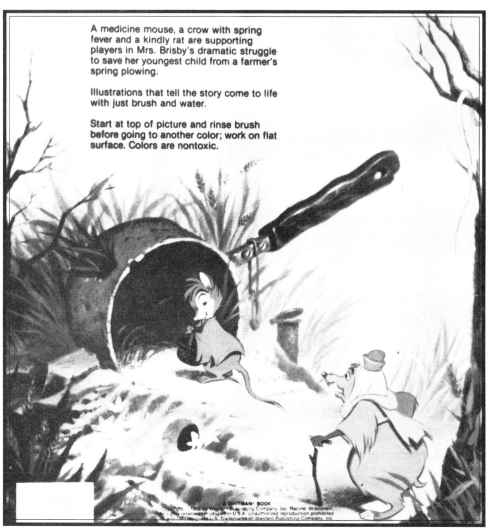

A medicine mouse, a crow with spring fever and a kindly rat are supporting players in Mrs. Brisby's dramatic struggle to save her youngest child from a farmer's spring plowing.

Illustrations that tell the story come to life with just brush and water.

Start at top of picture and rinse brush before going to another color; work on flat surface. Colors are nontoxic.

A WHITMAN® BOOK

You can see if you really are looking for it and you know what to look for. The overall look of Disney's *Snow White* was beautiful, but there were some sequences that had some pretty sloppy painting in it. It just depended who had their hand to it.

Q:
What is an average daily routine in this job?

Q:
Do you have a specific number you're trying to do every day?
A:
If you're doing keys for production work where you're going to be actually in control of the people who are going to be interpreting your keys, they [the keys] can be loose and basically, color studies that you can hand to an

artist. And as they develop their painting, you can direct it. In our particular case, here at TV Disney Animation, we're sending it overseas. So I don't have that luxury of being able to control what they're going to do with my keys, so we have to be pretty explicit with what we put down on paper, and so therefore, it takes longer to do the keys.

Usually a key takes a day-and-a-half to two days because, generally, the keys that we're dealing with are the most elaborate scenes in the movie. You're not going to key a simple wall card. It's not necessary. You'll key the entire room that that wall is included in. So you end up with furniture and curtains and just miles and miles of rendering that establishes the room and everything in it. Then, the production people, they'll do things that maybe have just one chair in it and they can do those quicker. So, on production backgrounds, you may be able to do three, four, five a day, depending on the subject that you're dealing with. But in keys, it's usually a day-and-a-half to two days. There are exceptions when you get larger ones that have whole cities in them. Sometimes they run to three days.

Q:

How much freedom are you given on an average production?

A:

Basically, after talking with the director and getting a general idea, unless he has a very specific thing in mind color-wise like, "I want this to be blue," it's pretty much up to me what I want to paint, as long as it's attractive and states the moment that's trying to be achieved. There's quite of bit of freedom from that aspect.

Q:

Which do you prefer keying for: Saturday morning TV or features?

A:

Well, I prefer keying for features. Fortunately, at this point in time, the keying that I'm doing for this Saturday morning, they want quality in their keys, hopefully to stimulate the foreign production people to bring their quality up. The idea being that if you give them something with more quality, then they're going to have to espouse more interest in themselves to try and reach that plateau. If you give them something that's just simply done, they have nothing to reach for and they'll give you about half of what you give them. So if you give them a weak key, then you're going to get half of it back. If you give them a strong key, many times, they'll give you over half. If they're challenged by something, they try to achieve it just to maintain their own dignity and their own self-esteem.

I've been overseas several times and there are some good painters over there and they're generally not challenged. But when they were challenged, they did come up to the challenge. Consequently, the keys that I'm doing for the shows that I've been on, they're like feature keys, atmospheric painting, so I've been comfortable with that. So that's one reason why I have remained here and not in features.

Q:

What production have you worked on that gave you the most personal satisfaction?

BACKGROUND

A:

It's hard to say. Probably *American Tail*. It was an interesting project. There was a lot of experimentation we did with effects and key background work in that, that was interesting. We were trying to do something different. *The Secret of Nimh* was interesting also. But I came in on the background end of *The Secret of Nimh* later on. Initially, I was doing production things like designing box wraps and things like that. I was also doing storyboards, coloring storyboards for the Leica reel. As we finished the animation, the board pieces were replaced on the reel. Then I did some of the backgrounds towards the end. But that was enjoyable just being part of that process.

Q:

What would you say was a product that you worked on that you don't think lived up to what you were hoping for?

A:

It's hard to say. I guess you kind of bury those things (laughs). It's like pain, do you remember how you felt the last time you had pain? Your mind kind of blocks out the painful experiences. Basically, there's nothing that I've really worked on that I could say was a failure, other than some jobs required excruciating hours that I would've liked not to have put in. But I really don't feel I've done anything that I could attribute to being a failure anyway. All the jobs have been interesting in some way. And that's partially, probably attributable to attitude, too.

If you go in and try to make the best of everything you do, and if you paint for yourself, the project works itself out some-how. You gain some knowledge and experience out of the project no matter whether it was a failure, or the group that you were working with was a failure or not, you've gained something. So it's important that you bring your own attitude into the situation and make the best of whatever you're doing.

Q:

If you were beginning today in the business with background or key painting, how would you prepare yourself?

A:

Beginning today, it would be very difficult, mainly because most everything is done overseas. So there's no real apprentice program nowadays. In the past, back in the Sixties and Seventies, almost all the TV animation productions were done here. They had larger crews and quicker production, so you could start there as an apprentice. They were more forgiving in taking you in because you weren't going to be doing keying. You were going to be doing production backgrounds. You're not going to mess up a wall card too badly. And they needed those hands to do wall cards so their better artists could do the more complicated paintings.

Consequently, by being there and just doing the simple paintings, you were learning by observing. But now, they don't have that because it's all sent overseas. Where do you apprentice in this business? It takes years to become a key person. They're skipping a whole sequence of learning.

We have interns that come here from colleges in the East and they say, "We want to do animation so badly. How do we get in?" I say, "I can't tell you," because most everyone working here in our division are all experienced people. They have to have the knowledge behind what they're doing so that it can be interpreted overseas and not misinterpreted. That takes a lot of experience to know what to put down and how much to put down.

Schooling-wise, you should get a really good art education. Perhaps Cal Arts, they do animation there. You might have a better chance if you've been to Cal Arts because of the fact that they do have a very specific animation school there. We pick up some artists out of [Pasadena] Art Cen-

background painting, but it's not like an ongoing thing where every week they hire somebody. When they have a feature going and they get an overload of work and need someone, they will hire apprentices to come in and help out. There are also some smaller studios that you could go to that do production work that you might have a chance of getting in.

AN
AMERICAN
TALE

© Universal

ter that have strong portfolios.

Disney still does their feature work here for the most part. They hire people as apprentices in

BACKGROUND

*Phil Phillipson
has been a fix-
ture in back-
ground paint-
ing for more
than a dec-
ade. His back-
ground of
working in al-
most all as-
pects of the
business gives
him a unique
feel for the
business. He's
done editorial
work (Pene-
lope Pitstop,
Scooby Doo,
Garfield and
Friends), assist-
ant animation
(Metamorpho
ses, The Black
Cauldron),
layouts (Fang
Face, The
Smurfs, Oliver
and Com-
pany), back-
grounds (Su-
perfriends,
Heavy Metal,
Heidi's Song,
Family Dog,
The Great
Mouse De-
tective) and
color styling
(Mupper Ba-
bies, Bakshi's
Harlem Shuffle
video, Dun-
geons and
Dragons).
He's worked
at just about
every studio
from Hanna-
Barbera to
Bakshi to Dis-
ney. His efforts
include the
1989 smash hit
The Little Mer-
maid and
more recently
The Rescuers
Down Under.
We caught
Phil at a pri-
vate res-*

Phil Phillipson

DATE: JULY 16, 1990

Q:
*Please give a brief description
of your career, studios you've
worked for and productions
you've worked on.*
A:
Originally I wanted to draw
comic books. I've loved comic
books ever since I was 9 years
old. My dad gave me a George
Bridgeman anatomy book, and
that's what got the whole thing
started as far as art goes. From
that George Bridgeman book I
knew I wanted to be an artist
more than anything else in the
world, well, maybe a baseball
player (laughs).

With that Bridgeman book I
immediately discovered that
when you draw a hand, instead of
a circle with five little points
coming off it, there's all these an-

gles and intricate interlocking
wedges and blocks. From that
point comics were a natural pro-
gression where Bridgeman's
principles were being utilized.
Some of my favorite artists as a
kid were Jack Kirby, Joe Kubert,
Carmine Infantino, Gil Kane and
Mike Sekowsky. I was in High
School when I discovered Neal
Adams, Bernie Wrightson and
Jeff Jones and decided that's
what I wanted to do pro-
fessionally when I graduated.

I went to junior college and
took some art courses there. At
that time I was working in a hos-
pital, washing dishes, and a
friend says, "hey, you know if
you're interested in artwork why
don't you go to Hanna-Barbera?"
I had no idea who they were or
what animation was, but they
were only 20 miles away and that

Background from RESCUERS DOWN UNDER

was a lot closer than New York! I went down to Hanna-Barbera and applied. I didn't know what the job functions were and I said I just wanted to be an artist and they sort of laughed. They said, "What kind of artist?" I had no idea that there was Layout, Background, Animation, Xerox and film editing. I just wanted to draw.

The lady at the reception desk was very nice. She said, "Well, why don't you start in the mail room. That way you'll get exposure to all the other departments." They immediately hired me for the summer. I figured once you get a job you just keep working forever. I didn't realize what a layoff was (due to the fact a series does not go on forever). Of course, I was lucky in the mail room. They didn't get

layoffs because it was the cheapest paying job. I only made $2 an hour at that time in 1968.

I was in the mail room for about six months when I got my first break doing editorial work for Larry Cowan. My first promotion was to track reader. That's where you break down the mouth assignments for the animator on the exposure sheets. After that I was constantly bugging Iwao Takamoto [major stylist for Hanna-Barbera] for a job in layout. That was the closest thing that I could do as far as comic books go. My goals took a turn when I met an older gentlemen by the name of Paul Julian. It was Paul's brilliant backgrounds that opened my eyes to the infinite possibilities of color that totally changed my career goals from comics to painting.

So from editorial, which I was working full time at that time, from 1968 to 1972 I was always bugging Iwao for a job in layout and finally I got my first chance in 1973 on *Inch High Private Eye*. From that, because it was a busy season, I got a chance to go into background. From that point I worked at Hanna-Barbera off and on because of the various layoffs.

Starting in 1976 I began moving out of Hanna-Barbera into various other studios. The first non-H.B. Studio was Sanrio, where I was an assistant animator. That was my first theatrical film. Other studios I worked at were Ralph Bakshi's, dePatie-Freleng, Ruby-Spear, Columbia, Filmation, back to Hanna-Barbera and all around town.

I came to Disney in 1983 on *The Black Cauldron* as an assistant animator. Again, trying to break in as a painter. Through these various careers I was taking night classes at Art Center from 1971 through 1978. In 1985 I got a chance to work at Disney as a background painter exclusively.

Q:

What tools do you work with?

A:

The brushes that I personally like and use are Brumbacher number 6142, Aqua-rel. I use the half-inch, three-quarter-inch and one-inch chisel brush. My round head brushes are Isabee special series Colinski, 6227Z and I use the number fours, sixes and eights. Most of my work is done with those brushes. Very rarely will I deviate from those unless there's a special project or a special technique that's employed and I have to follow. But basically those brushes will carry me through anything.

Q:

What sort of paints do you generally use?

A:

Saturday morning studios were basically using vinyl acrylic paints. That's acrylic with vinyl, which has a plastic base to it. It's very permanent. It doesn't fade, doesn't bleed or anything, it's just forever.

Disney had their own special paint department that blended their own pigment. It was like gauche or tempera. It was not permanent so that if you spilled your coffee or your water on it, it would disturb the surface, whereas vinyl acrylic you could spill coffee on it and it wouldn't do anything to it. You just wipe it up like a vinyl floor.

Q:

On Saturday morning and feature films, the first step in doing backgrounds is establishing what they call a color key.

A:

Yes. Color keys use color to design and style a particular locale. The studio or project will determine how abbreviated or fully rendered each key will be. Depending on the amount of freedom each studio allows its BG department determines if a supervisor or each painter gets to do his or her own keys. From the keys each painter than prepares his background as camera ready artwork. Each process has its own individual challenge.

Features are generally more muted using very subtle hues and values. Saturday morning on the other hand has to pump up the chroma, hue, and values across the board to compensate for all the generations that will take place before broadcast. The steps being film to tape to broadcast and the final kicker *your* TV set. Everyone's TV seems to be adjusted slightly different from everyone else's.

Theatrically, the key word is control. Theater screens don't have scan lines and all are basically the same, except for size. Therefore you can get those muted grays, you get those subtle values and harmonies of color that you can appreciate. The TV just doesn't pick it up. Or if it does pick it up it just doesn't do it justice

Q:
Can you give examples of films with good backgrounds?
A:

Yes, *Bambi*, *Lady and the Tramp*, *Pinocchio*, all those old Disney classics. Those were some of the most gorgeous backgrounds ever painted. And it's very interesting about those backgrounds. I've had a chance to go to the Disney morgue and see them up close and they don't look at all like they do on film. They're still very beautiful backgrounds and very well painted. The surprise from seeing them up close is that you realize immediately that they were painted for film, not as illustrations.

There's two schools of thought concerning background painting, and that is painting versus rendering. The rendering school wants to achieve ultimate realism which does not heighten the sense of bigger than life or fantasy of a particular scene.

The painting school is more impressionistic and deals a little more with values of lights and darks placed next to each other. That's the key thing you'll see in the old Disney backgrounds when you finally get a chance to see them up close. The painting

ability of those painters was incredible and second to none. They were paintings as opposed to renderings.

Q:
What's the difference between a painting and a rendering?
A:

To simplify it, let's say you have an example of a house, with a wood shingle roof. The rendering of the roof will have each shingle delineated, light, medium and dark. A painting will have one light brush stroke placed next to a dark brush stroke so that when the pattern is repeated it will create an impression of realism using a painterly system.

A rendering when held in front of you, will look very similar to a book illustration. It will look beautiful. The craftsmanship will be exemplary. On the other hand, a painting in front of you might not look so good because it's being held out of context. You also have to consider screen time, the preceding scene and the succeeding scene.

When a director's notes call for a particular scene to be two feet long, a little over a second and a half, which is a blink of an eye. A painting holds up during screen time, or a director's timing, better than a rendering. A painting will have the immediacy of the light and the dark, as opposed to a rendering where you have subtle nuances that no one will ever see except for the person holding it in front of him.

Q:
How do you go about converting a layout into a final background or a production background?
A:

I transfer it with graphite

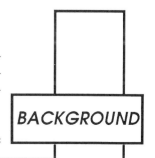

BACKGROUND

paper. It's similar to carbon paper, but rather than carbon, its coating is just like your graphite pencil. You put that underneath the layout and then you transfer the image with a stylus, which looks like a fine-point needle, onto your background board.

The background board is usually Strathmore, cold press, hundred pound weight. Sometimes they'll go three hundred pound weight. The only difference is it's a little bit thicker backing. But as far as the surface that we paint on, it's equal. There's no difference there. The Strathmore board is a little bit nicer as far as preservation goes, an archival-type quality. Now, at Hanna-Barbera where I started we didn't have that. It was like a Strathmore two-ply. It's what a comic book artist would use, like bristle board. It was thinner. When it got wet, it was like a potato chip. You had to mount it onto a board as opposed to being on a board from the beginning.

Q:

How do you actually paint a production or key background.

A:

Use the comparison between Saturday morning and theatrical. Both processes are approximately the same. The only difference is that in Saturday morning you'll probably have a little bit more liberty and freedom to do what you want. You can probably assert yourself artistically more than you can in a theatrical where you have to more or less follow closely the people you're working with. But you make up for it by having enough time to do the absolute best job you can.

Theatrically if you've got four people or 20 people painting backgrounds, they're all sup-posed to look like one person painted the product. Now, on Saturday morning that still holds true. Although along with following the general style like on *Scooby Doo,* you could always experiment. And that was more or less encouraged because you're compensating for lack of animation. When something looked striking value-wise or color-wise it was encouraged to go with it. In a theatrical you're trying to use subtle hues and values because you'll be able to see the subtlety. Theatrically the animation is dominant so you don't have to compensate with harsh values and hues. Each has its own discipline and each is fun to paint in its own way

Q:

After you've transferred the layout onto the background board, how do you actually get down to physically starting it?

A:

Always start like the namesake. You start in the background first and then come forward to the foreground. So you go background, middle ground, foreground. You do the things furthest away from the foreground, like the sky or clouds, then you come forward from the mountain. The furthest mountain range up to the closest mountain range, then to the foreground where your main characters stand.

Q:

Who, on an average day in production, do you generally work with?

A:

Theatrically, where I'm at right now at Disney, we have a background department and the work is disbursed from our supervisor. They will take portions of a sequence and divide it up amongst the department and they would then give either one layout or several layouts, depending on how fast the work needs to be done.

I'll take that layout and go back to my desk, usually in the morning, and set my station up. To accommodate that particular layout I'll go to the file drawer and find other backgrounds in that particular section that have been painted. If there are none then the supervisor will probably give me a small color key to follow. At that point I will interpret those colors either color for color or I will have to extrapolate the mood of that particular scene and then proceed to paint it. After I've acquired all my research material from the file cabinet, I will then go back to my desk and start to paint it.

Q:
Are you checked on by anybody as you progress?
A:

Yes. Usually at the very beginning of a movie there'll be a lot of experimentation. You can try different styles. The art director or the directors will decide if it's hitting the mark or not. That's usually the most fun because you get to experiment. Then as the production progresses it gets finely tuned and finally there is no more experimentation. Depending at what period in the production I'm in, will determine how much research I require. Toward the end of the production there is lots to choose from. Therefore, the research acquiring portion of the day is very minimal, if any at all.

Q:
What projects have you worked on that you've really enjoyed and why?
A:

Roger Rabbit. It's a real toss up between *Roger* and *Little Mermaid.* The reason why *Roger* gets the nod is purely from a creative standpoint. *Roger*'s the only Disney production where I was called in on the very beginning of a project and asked to design in color. But because I was already assigned to another feature, I had to do Toon Town at night, after hours. That caused the time schedule to become strained. Because of the crunch, they needed someone else, so they called in my brother, Andy Phillipson. It was great working with Andy as co-designers on *Roger.* Unfortunately, two people doing work at night still wasn't enough. (Andy was also involved with another project during the day.) They were lucky enough to get Ron Dias full time and the rest, as they say, is history. Andy and I didn't receive any film credit, but we had the satisfaction of being in at the beginning of one of the greatest movies of all time.

Conversely, *Mermaid,* my other favorite, was second only because the work I did do on it was of a following nature; implement and execute other designers' work. This carries a different type of satisfaction, though.

The biggest conflict I have with myself is how powerful my contribution is measured against how good the project materializes. It's like being on a team. You may have a great game with terrific stats but the team loses. That's not good. Or you're on an all-star team and they blow out the league, but you didn't contribute very much. That's not satisfying either. The ideal is to do

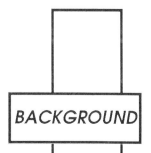

BACKGROUND

great work on a great project. That's the combination I'm always striving for.

Q:

How would you tell someone to prepare for getting into the animation industry?

A:

If I knew what I know now back then I would've gone to art school right out of high school. That's the best training. Art Center School of Design in Pasadena or Cal Arts are the two best schools for art in this area.

Unfortunately, all Saturday morning production is now done overseas, leaving a huge void for gaining experience. The way I started you wouldn't be able to duplicate; being an apprentice and learning from a master.

Background from HEAVY METAL

© Columbia Pictures

Chris Buck is one of the newer breed of animators, having begun his career in the late Seventies. He quickly established himself as a top animator and has been in demand ever since. His talent has aided Disney features, commercials, Warner Brothers shorts and now prime time TV series. He also has taught animation at Cal Arts.
This interview took place in a trailer on the Amblin' lot at Universal Studios, where Chris directs the Family Dog prime time series. Since then, the Family Dog unit has moved to a spacious office building in downtown Glendale.

Chris Buck

DATE: JULY 27, 1990

Q:
Please give us a brief description of your varied career.
A:
Well, I guess I'll start with the schooling. I started by going to Cal Arts for two years. At the end of each year, they have a special producers' show for the people at Disney to view the student films. I was hired after the 1978 show, and started at Disney that summer as a trainee.

I began as an inbetweener on *The Fox and the Hound*, and worked my way up to assistant during that picture, by doing a personal pencil test. I became an animator to help out with the titles for that picture, doing scenes of the mother running with the baby fox.

After that we did a short, *Fun with Mr. Future*, which was originally planned for an Epcot TV show. They ended up scrapping the whole concept, so we slugged together a lot of animation to make a short. Next, Mike Giaimo, Darrell van Citters and I did some experimental footage and character designs for *Roger Rabbit*, with Darrell directing. I worked just briefly on *Mickey's Christmas Carol*, then did one scene on *The Black Cauldron*, and then I left Disney. That was in 1984.

During this leave of absence, I did commercials, starting with Film Fair. I worked with Tim Burton, doing boarding on *Frankenweenie*, a live action featurette, that he's re-editing for Disney right now. From there, I went back to Disney to work with Darrell on *Sport Goofy*.

100

Then I joined Brad Bird to do the original *Family Dog* , for *Amazing Stories*, which took me through the end of 1986. I went back to commercials after *Dog*, at Kurtz and Friends, and eventually did some freelance for Disney. I didn't go back in-house, though. I was still a little leery of them after my last experience there. I did some character designs for *The Little Mermaid* then back to Kurtz, and then back to Disney for some experimental animation and character designs on *Rescuers Down Under*.

In early 1989 I joined Darrell and Mike again, over at Warner Brothers Classics, to bring back Bugs Bunny in a short, *Box Office Bunny*. There was also a lot of publicity work for Bugs' fiftieth. After finishing up on that, I came over here to direct the *Family Dog* series. That'll be 13 episodes for CBS' prime time next spring.

Q:
What commercials did you work on?
A:
There were several Keeblers. It was ironic that, during my first stretch at Disney, I had never done their classic characters. On my first commercial at Film Fair I did Mickey, Donald and Goofy for some soft drink. There was a Rocky and Bullwinkle for Hershey's Kisses, several years ago, with Sam Cornell.

Q:
What does an animator do?
A:
Well, there's the old cliche of being an actor with a pencil, and

Ursula, the sea witch in THE LITTLE MERMAID. Preliminary design

© Walt Disney Co

bringing the drawings to life. These are both true, but the animator's real challenge is to put something of himself into the character. You hope that character will remain in the audience's head for a while, and not just be forgotten as soon as the credits roll.

There's a lot more to good animation than nice drawings. If you have great drawings and bad timing, you're lost. I've seen a lot of great draftsmen, who lack the timing and acting sense, and their work suffers on the screen. On the other hand, if you have good timing and acting, you could have an entertaining film with stick figure drawings. If you're lucky, you'll have a good assistant, who'll make it look good.

Q:

What would you consider examples of good animation?

A:

I really enjoyed *The Little Mermaid* . They did a nice job on that. In good animation you see control. The animator has to learn to control himself, to see the big picture and know when to go broad and when to pull back and be more subtle. There needs to be a balance of motion. A lot of animators, myself included, are guilty of going off with a scene, and making it fun to watch all by itself, but when it's added to the rest of the project, it just doesn't fit. There's a lot of new stuff that's very high energy, but it's just over the top all the time, and watching even 10 minutes of it drives me nuts. There's so much going on, I don't know what to watch.

Animation also suffers with weak stories. *All Dogs Go to Heaven* was one of those. There

a lot of talented people over at Bluth, and it was sad to see all that talent and hard work go to waste on a story that just wasn't up to their abilities.

I love *The Simpsons*. They're great scripts with some quirky animation to fit.

The old Warner cartoons, and of course a couple of the Disney classics. *Pinocchio* is still my favorite. It was beautifully animated, with a warm story, and lots of heart to the characters. If you're going to invest 70 minutes in watching a feature, you should come away with some lasting feelings—something more than being mildly amused.

Bambi also works on a visual level more than others. It relies more on visuals than on dialogue, and its animation was flawless.

Cauldron, on the other hand, was a mess. It went through so many hands. That picture had a lot of blood on it and it showed. It showed that there really wasn't a focus at the time. They were searching for something. Disney's found something now. I think they're back on track.

Q:

What is an example of poor animation?

A:

Roger Rabbit. As I was involved at the beginning, it's hard for me to be objective. I envisioned something different; a character with more heart. Roger turned out so obnoxious that I couldn't like him. They were going for a Tex Avery/Warner Brothers look, but the best of Warner's animation is still controlled. They [Warners] knew how to do the zany stuff, and when to pause to let that pay off. Again, that's pacing and timing. *Roger* was very hard to watch.

Trying to keep up with it literally gave me a headache.

Bluth is guilty of the same thing. His stuff is all over the place, too. Today, people seem to think full animation means animation that's moving all the time. Animation can use holds and still be full.

Q:
How do you approach animating a new character?
A:

When I've gotten a new character to animate. I've usually been lucky enough to have had a hand in designing him. In general, an animator will take the design he's given and adapt it as he gets into it. The design will evolve as the character's personality comes out, and as certain problems with moving him show up.

I start out by researching the character, finding out who he is within the story, what his role is. Should he be broader than the rest? He has to work with the whole picture. Then I'll look for other performances that remind me of the one I'm developing. Not other animation. I look to live action characters, even if its an animal I'm working on. I'll study animal footage for movement, and human performances for personality and acting. Animators ripping off previous animation for these things have made the industry incestuous. The product just becomes a hybrid and ends up looking gross.

I'll also ask other animators how they see the character, to get some more perspective. After the research, before I even get a scene, I just start playing with poses to learn how to draw him. Once the scenes are handed out, I'll listen to the voice. That will dictate a lot about the character, whether his movements are sharp or slow.

Then I just get into the scenes, and it keeps evolving as we go. By the end of the picture, you finally know how to draw the character, and who he is, but then it's over.

Q:
What is your daily routine?
A:

My job is to sit down at my desk for eight hours and try to get into the character, into the scene, and bring that character to life. I'll do a lot of tests. I'm up at the video a lot, trying to get my timing to work. First I rough out the main poses, and shoot that on the video. Then, if the scene has a track, I'll play that along with the video to see if the attitudes are working. That gives me a skeleton to work with. I look at animation as sculpting. You start out with a big lump of clay, and you keep taking away and adding bits until you've fine tuned it into an entertaining little piece.

Q:
How much freedom are you given on an average production?
A:

That depends on whether you're a directing animator or not. They have the most freedom. Then also, different studios work differently. Disney is fairly open. They'd hand you a blank exposure sheet and say, "Here, you've got a second and a half. Make it funny." Other places you may be given exactly how many frames to do a jump or a hold. That is actually a help sometimes, since its tough to read a director's mind. Commercials are usually pretty tight, because

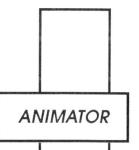

ANIMATOR

there's so much information to get into a small amount of time.

Q:

What have been some of your favorite characters to animate?

A:

I enjoyed Gerta LaStrange. She was an offbeat character in the original *Family Dog*. I enjoyed almost all the characters in *Family Dog*. They were fun to do.

Q:

You enjoy fun characters?

A:

Basically, yes. It's very hard for me to get into the more human characters that they're doing today. Very hard. It bothers me that animation is getting more realistic. I mean, why do it in animation?

Q:

What other characters have you not enjoyed working on?

A:

Sport Goofy. The whole concept of the character was created by merchandising, as a co-ordinated athletic talent. And the true character of Goofy is dimwitted, clumsy and uncoordinated. That's his whole schtick. That's the fun of him. So we were stuck trying to give the old design a new character. It never did work for me.

Q:

What project that you were involved with has given you the most professional satisfaction, or enjoyment?

A:

For professional enjoyment, I'd have to say *Family Dog*. I got to help out in a lot of areas, and I think we achieved something that hadn't been done on television

for quite a while. We brought back nice full, character-oriented animation to TV. I liked the fact that the dog didn't talk. In a lot of today's animation all the animals talk and they're up on two legs running around, like humans in animal suits. We tried to keep this dog a *dog*, yet he was still caricatured. He wasn't realistic. The fact that he didn't talk was even more challenging. We had to make the acting tell the story, rather than talking through it in dialogue.

Working with Brad [Bird] was very helpful. He pushed me to go a little further, to reach for the performance he wanted. It was really his vision that brought the project together so well. It was a real challenge, but very satisfying.

Q:

Is there a project that you worked on that you felt failed?

A:

Besides *Roger Rabbit*? *Mickey's Christmas Carol*. From day one, I thought, "Why do it?" They didn't have a fresh angle on it to make it interesting. They were just slugging in Mickey, Donald and Goofy. I think they only came up with the idea because it had been a story album first. Merchandising again. Anyway, *Christmas Carol* is such a great story, and it's been done well, so many different ways, if you're going to animate it, why not do something original, something really special with it. Mickey, Donald and Goofy just didn't plus it any.

Q:

If you were to advise someone on how to get into the industry today, what would you tell them?

A:

Along with the obvious courses, like life drawing, perspective, and basic animation, I'd tell them to be sure to take some art history and filmmaking courses. I'm still playing catch-up on those. The art history gives you a broader perspective, a greater appreciation of other artists, other art forms. It's something to refer to.

The principles of good filmmaking apply to animation, as well. Studying live action films can open an animator up to thinking about a wider variety of camera angles and unique staging. Medium shots, one after another, get boring. It begins to feel like a puppet show with just talking heads. Animation alone can get pretty myopic. It's easy to get caught up in your own scene and lose sight of the whole picture.

I try to stress to the students that they should really enjoy the creative freedom they have while they're at school, and not be just champing at the bit to get out into the business world. Because as soon as they're out, they'll be doing someone else's vision.

It's important to be able to find some personal enjoyment in every stage of the game. A lot of people start off as inbetweeners who moan and groan, and on and on, until they become a director, and still you're doing somebody else's vision. You're doing what the producer sees, what the head of the studio sees, what the distributors want. So, enjoy being your own director while you're in school, and then try to hang on to your love of the art form, your love of entertainment. Hang onto that when you're doing the projects that you don't like, they're inevitable. Then, enjoy the ones you can while you're on them. That's a survival skill in itself.

Roger Rabbit and Jessica in a 1982 design

© Walt Disney Co.

ANIMATOR

Mark Kausler, for almost two decades, lived the life of a freelance animator. Based at no studio, he would pick up animation work wherever and whenever it was available. This meant he experienced working at more studios, with more variety of talent, than most people in the business his age. His resume includes some of the most famous animated characters in history, from Daffy Duck to Tony the Tiger to Roger Rabbit. As he entered his third decade in the industry, he settled at the Disney studio working on such projects as Roller Coaster Rabbit and Mickey's Prince and the Pauper.
We talked with Mark at his home, a veritable archive of animation. Mark is one of the most respected animation history authorities in the business. His name is found in the acknowledge

Mark Kausler

DATE:: JULY 28, 1990

Q:
Could you please give a brief description of your career, including the studios you've worked at, and the productions you've worked on?
A:
Well, let me see. I started in 1968, working at studios like Filmation and an old studio called Fred Calvert Productions, which no longer exists. He was doing freelance work for Jay Ward. We did a little segment of *Yellow Submarine* there. Then the next year I worked for John Wilson's company, Fine Arts Films, on *Shinbone Alley*. And then shortly after that, after I graduated from school which was in 1970, I worked for Spungbuggy Works for two years as an animator.

Learned a lot there about the nuts and bolts of the business and how to put together a commercial.

I got to design and animate some, what we call, "animatics." They're like pose reels, really. We did some for Esso Gas that were the Krazy Kat, Herriman style. For those I got to work right on paper with a felt tip pen and do all the cross-hatching, cut them out and paste them on the cels and do all the coloring. Did the backgrounds. Did everything. Those were so much fun because I got to do the entire process. I even picked out the sound effects.

After a while I jumped out of Spungbuggy and freelanced. I worked at various shops for a year or two each, like Duck Soup, Pacific Motion Pictures (now called West Indigo) and

Warner Brothers. All the standard Leo Burnett-type stuff: Tony the Tiger and dozens of Fruit Loops commercials.

I guess my favorite commercials that I ever worked on were Popeye Video games, for Pacific Motion Pictures. We got a chance to do the old Segar-type Popeye. It was against these live action sets and the result almost had the feel of the old Fleischer 3-D. That was really fun. Some of the last stuff that Jack Mercer voiced were for those spots. Those really stand out in my mind.

I'm forgetting a lot of stuff like Ralph Bakshi. I went in and picked up several segments of *Heavy Traffic* and *Coon Skin* and just did those at home and brought in the finished art. And it goes on and on. (Laugh) I should

have looked at my old freelance record books. Lot of this stuff I'm happy to have forgotten! Oh, one special I worked on that I wonder if anybody remembers was *Clero Wilson and the Miracle of P.S. 14*, which was an early Flip Wilson show. Corny Cole directed it at DePatie-Freleng. I didn't like the results on that one at all.

Even if I worked in-house at a studio, I always made sure I was paid as self-employed. I was freelance for 17 years. Then I got hired at Disney, actually by Amblin, to work on *Who Framed Roger Rabbit* [he helped board the film and among other things animated Droopy]. I'm now officially at Disney where I recently worked on *Tummy Trouble*, *Roller Coaster Rabbit* and *Mickey's Prince and the Pauper*.

Q:

What, if any, actual art training do you have?

A:

I went four years to art schools. I went two years in Kansas City to Kansas City Art Institute. I thought I was going to be a painter. I was studying fine art and lithography. I love lithography. That was 1966, 1968. In 1968, I came out here and got a scholarship to Chouinard with the help of T. Hee [famous Disney storyman] and was there two years from 1968 to 1970. Then I graduated with a B.F.A. in 1970.

Q:

How did you break into the business?

A:

Well, I didn't even think I could do it. I loved cartoons ever since I was eight, but my mother always said, "You'll never break in. Forget it."

I came out here [Los Angeles] to visit friends of mine, like Manon Washburn, who were in animation. Manon was an inker and she introduced me to a guy named Gary Mooney. He was an animator over at the old Quartet Films, which I think still exists. Gary said, "Well, if you really think you can do it I've got some rough inbetweens I want you to do." It was the Green Giant. I said, "Yeah, I'll try it." So I tried it and I thought they were horrible but he thought they were usable. So with those samples, just three inbetweens I did on the Green Giant, I went to Filmation. I Just walked in right off the street and showed them to Hal Sutherland. He said, "Start Monday." He didn't even want to talk at great length.

So I came in, I think they were paying 80 bucks a week in those days. I was called an assistant animator, but at Filmation you really were more of a Xerox machine operator. The shows that were going in Filmation then were *Aquaman*, *Batman*, a few episodes of *Superman* because they'd already done two years and these were just little additional episodes. Tons of "Archies" stuff. *Archie* was the most fun. Everybody wanted to work on *Archie* . Especially anything that had Hot Dog in it, because Hot Dog was a cartoony character. We enjoyed drawing Hot Dog. Everything else was an utter chore.

The only people who drew well at Filmation were the layout people. A lot of times you didn't even have time to draw Batman or Aquaman. You just took the layouts, Xeroxed two of them, ripped off the legs, ripped off the arms and literally repositioned them, like cut-out animation. Make a new Xerox of that, strip it up and hand it in. We were under tremendous pressure.

Here I was totally green. It was my first summer out here, I didn't know what the heck I was doing and (chuckle) I had to turn out 200 feet a week. One day, I was working really hard. I was really worried, "Am I going to survive here? What am I going to do?" [Norm] Prescott, Lou Scheimer, Hal Sutherland, the Terrible Threesome, walked into my room. They all pointed to me and said, "More footage," turned on their heels and walked out. I think they were probably just doing it for a gag. But it really made me nervous. I was really scared.

I was very glad to go back to school after that. They tried to talk me into staying at Filmation. I said, "No." T. Hee really encouraged me to go back to school. He said, "Don't just fall into the business right away. You should get schooling. You'll be better off in the long run." I think he was right.

Q:

What does an animator do?

A:

An animator basically tells a story. He makes it work on film. Your raw material is storyboards or scripts that usually somebody else has written. But it's the animator's basic responsibility to make it work, to communicate to the audience through movement, or just through a single drawing, the attitude that the story is supposed to convey. I think that's the basic definition of what an animator's job is: communication!

Q:

Can you give me some examples of what you think are films or TV shows or shorts that have good animation versus those that would have bad animation.

A:

I guess some of my favorite animation would be some of the old shorts, like some of the Warner Brothers stuff, of course Bob Clampett's cartoons. The Rod Scribner animation is great. He made the story points so funny by the way he moved the characters and by the way his drawing looks. His drawing is so funny. From the start you laugh just at the way it looks. And then the gags are there to support it. I think he did a wonderful job of taking the material that he was supplied with, which was probably pretty raw, judging from the storyboards I've seen from Clampett's cartoons, they're pretty

rough, and just turning it into entertainment. So good at it.

And then Irv Spence on the Tom and Jerry's. that was great animation. The way he could take just very raw scribbly stuff that Joe Barbera did and make it live. The timing that he had was so precise, the way it worked with the music, everything else, it's a total package. It's very smooth, it's very easy to watch and a lot of fun. And I don't want to belittle Disney features either, because all those guys were expert storytellers: Thomas, Johnston, Tytla, Babbit, Milt Kahl, Glen Keane, all the greats.

I love so many animators, it's hard to put it all into a nutshell. But I guess what I admire basically is somebody who can take the raw material, the storyboards, the script, whatever, and turn it into something better. Plus make it more entertaining. And really make the story live. They probably had to rewrite some lines to make it flow smoother or ask the director to cut some words so that it would have a more natural feeling. A lot of times, as you're animating, you discover that the writer has overwritten and you really have to pare it down in order for the audience to not only hear the dialogue but see your images. There's just so much people can absorb. I think a good animator has to be a good editor as well as a storyteller.

Oh, I didn't say anything about bad animation. That was good animation. Okay, bad animation, I guess is, I'm trying to think of the worst stuff I ever got, a lot of the stuff at Filmation, I guess is some of the worst stuff ever done. Mainly because it's so cut and dried. And about 90 percent of the entertainment in Filmation's material is from the

ANIMATOR

track, like the *Star Trek* cartoons. They were such horrible animation, not even animation. It's a slide show. The only thing that makes it animated is they turn once in a while and their mouths move. I mean the only way it's entertaining is to listen. They actually make better radio shows than they would as cartoons.

Actually television shows, I guess have to be designed that way because a lot of the times people aren't even looking at the screen. They're serving dinner, they're running around the room, whatever. They're not really concentrating too hard. And television animation doesn't have to tell the story that much through the animation. It leans more heavily on the script and maybe just on a basic layout setup. If you have a good layout in television, that properly tells the story, it really doesn't have to move too much to put the point across. To me that's bad animation because the animation isn't helping tell the story or put the point across.

What else is bad animation? *Clutch Cargo* is pretty bad. That's everybody's classic example because they didn't even have the budget to animate the mouths, they had them filmed live action and superimposed over the heads. A lot of people think Terry Toons are examples of bad animation. Maybe the animation isn't as much the problem as it's the material the animators have to work with. There were some very good animators at Terry Toons, like Jim Tyer, and some very creative people. But the material they had to work with was just third rate. It was just formula stuff. A lot of people complained about the Famous Studios' Casper the Ghost, and

Baby Huey's. But Marty Taras, Dave Tendlar, some of those guys were excellent animators. Some of the best guys that ever worked. But their material was hackneyed, it was second rate Tom and Jerry scripts. Cookie cutter. They always had the same plot and just substituted different details. Which is essentially the way a lot of TV series are done today. Once you get a plot that works, just substitute the details and presto, you got another episode. We could talk for hours about this.

Q:
As an animator, how do you approach animating a new character?

A:
With a new character you try to think of things that you might have seen before. Either in animation or live action or animals you know or people you know that might help you in getting characteristics for this character. If you're animating a new dog character, what kind of a dog is it? Is it a bulldog, is it a Chihuahua, light, heavy, vicious, kind? You have to get the basic character traits down. Then you try to particularize. You try to go from the general to the specific, to make a unique character out of it.

Like when we were working on *Oliver and Company.* I thought Tito was an interesting and funny character. I thought he was kind of a fun character because of his voice and because he's a lot like the street gang members that roam around Los Angeles. He was sort of like a gang member, a little bit of a new wrinkle in animation. It made his character more interesting than just doing another Mexican Chihuahua, which is a stereotype. You're taking the stereotype and making it more interesting by making the caricature a specific person. I kind of enjoyed that aspect of the character.

Q:

What about an established character that you're working on for the first time?

A:

Well, in the case of Daffy Duck, the first scene I ever got of him, I went to existing animation. I would get it out of the library and look at it a lot. I would make a lot of drawings, just exploration drawings, to see whether I could handle him or not. You make a lot of little sketches, just fooling around for shapes. See if you can draw the bill. What the attitudes are in the character. And that was a great help just looking at pre-existing stuff.

But then, you have the horrible responsibility of taking these great animators like McKimson, Scribner, Ben Washam and take their stuff and put your own experience on it too. You sort of re-interpret their stuff through your hands and your eyes. It's not easy to live up to. It's a very difficult task. I think maybe it's more satisfying to take something that's a new character nobody's ever seen and just try to animate it to the best of your ability, like Roger Rabbit. He was so much fun for me to do because he was a collection of bits and pieces of all characters and all experience. He's such a total idiot, a brainless idiot, that you don't have the complex personality problems you might have with another character. And for me, he was just a delight to do. I enjoyed working on him.

Q:

Let's talk about the actual work. What is a daily routine for an animator?

A:

Well, you wake up in the morning. (laugh) You try to avoid eating as much as you can because you sit down all day at a desk. What is it? "A second on the lips, a lifetime on the hips!" You can get heavy real easy. So I have to watch what I eat. Usually just have a cup of coffee or something like that. You wake up, walk around a little bit and do a couple of exercises and go to work.

The first thing I would do is just look at the layouts a lot. If I'm starting on a new scene I listen to the track, if there's a track on cassette of the character's voice, 30, 40 times. Then I look at the exposure sheet I'm given and I circle words that seem to be the most important words to hit. That's your key. Usually the sound track will guide you, if there is one, to what's the most important points in the scene to hit. When I circle those words I know that's where I've got to make my emphasis.

Then I'll make thumbnail sketches, a lot of them. Usually they look like little storyboards but they're not really storyboards, they're an animator's breakdown of the storyboard. Maybe you'll do a sketch for every frame, or every sixth frame. However many it takes to put the point across. That's maybe how I start a scene.

I'll talk to the director maybe every two to three days. I'll show him the thumbnails; he'll approve those. Then I'll work it up in rough. The way I work is I don't make my roughs like haystacks, like a lot of animators do.

ANIMATOR

This is because, when I was an assistant, I had to clean up Duane Crowther's roughs. Duane's a great animator but his roughs were really hard to clean up, but a great training in how a good animator thinks. Sometimes he would draw with a felt tip pen, sometimes he'd draw with a magic marker, I never knew what I was going to get next. You would have to take that and make it look a lot more like a character with a HB or a B pencil. And, oh, it's hard. It's really hard to interpret. So I always think about what the next person's going to get when I'm working on a drawing. I want to make it as succinct as I can, as clear as I can. So I draw a little bit cleaner maybe than the average animator does.

Then I will take those drawings and I'll either have somebody else do the rough inbetweens or if there's nobody around to do it, then I'll do it myself. Do all the rough inbetweens, then I shoot it on video tape and I show it to the director. Then I usually have to redo it. (chuckle) Even though the thumbnails pretty much spell out how you're going to do the scene, and the director approved it, a lot of times the director can't visualize what it's going to look like even when you've done your level best to show it to this person.

So then you have to go and take out hunks and murder your darlings. You really like the scene, it looks great. You show it to the director and he tears it apart. Then you have to make that psychological adjustment, which is sometimes not easy to do, and retool it, make it work, but not through your own brain. Somebody else's brain is controlling what you do. But it is a group effort, that's the big pain

of animation and the pleasure of it. It's not something somebody can do all by themselves. You really have to work with other people, it's just part of the business.

So that's a pretty typical day, and hopefully it's a day that lasts about eight hours. If you have to do tremendous amounts of overtime you get very, very tired. I think your time off in animation is just as important as your time on. A lot of times when you've worked around the house trying to clean stuff up or walk around the block or whatever, you're not even thinking about a scene, all of a sudden, "My God, why didn't I do it that way?" You think of a better thing to do, a better way to stage it, a better way to draw it, a word you should have hit, that you didn't hit in the track.

You'll go back to work the next day and throw out half your scene. But when you're always grinding away at it, working so hard trying to make the deadline, a lot of times you just settle for your second or third rate ideas because there's just no time to think. You just have to push out material.

Q:

How much freedom are you given on an average production?

A:

Well, when I was working commercials and on TV shows we didn't have very much freedom. What we were given were very tight storyboards. Usually drawn on model with all the background details indicated. Sometimes they were so clean you could make layouts from them. You'd just blow them up on a Xerox machine. Just redraw the background and make it tighter and redraw the characters.

In commercials we were always under the gun from the agency. What has happened is the studios, I guess in the early days of commercials, 1949 and 1950 and so forth, had more creative control. The agency didn't know what a television commercial was. But now so much time has gone by, so much experience, so many thousands of commercials have been made, they figured it out. The agencies have total control. Like when we we're doing' Fruit Loops' Toucan Sam or Tony the Tiger, the agency supplies model sheets. You have to be very precise about the way Tony's nose is drawn, the shape of his head, the way the toucan's bill is drawn, how many stripes are on it. You can really get bogged down in that. And it's a shame because I think better commercials could be made if they'd loosen up a little bit.

If the animators had a little bit more of a free rein to be able to tell the story a little better, I think you'd get better spots. But it's just the nature of commercials and television that it has to be tightly controlled because there's no time really to do it, and to experiment with it, and kick it back and forth. You usually have only two weeks to do an average 30-second spot. And that's considered a good schedule these days. Sometimes you only have a week, so it has to be pretty well tied down.

Even then you're going to get changes, and it's frustrating. A lot of the time you get silly changes. I remember one spot I worked on at Spungbuggy for Motorcraft Automotive Parts. We (chuckle) we had this little dump truck that this guy named Bob

Zoell designed. He used to be a pretty hot designer in the early Seventies. And (laugh) he had a little baseball cap on this truck's head. We had to take it off after we had already animated the whole thing. It had been approved, but the agency said his baseball cap might offend gas station attendants. Who knows why? That was their edict, so we had to take it off and change it to a red light.

Another silly change, on the same picture, was the hook on the back of the tow truck. It looked like a sickle. We had to change the design of the hook because the agency said it might offend people who had sickle-cell anemia. I said, "Boy, they really had to search for that one!" (Laugh) I couldn't believe it. So all that had to be redrawn.

Q:
What would you say have been some of your favorite characters and least favorite characters to animate and why?

A:
Well, I guess my favorite character that I've ever done so far is Roger Rabbit. Just because I followed him from beginning to end. I had a little bit of a hand in his design. I helped design his eyes, and worked with Dick Williams pretty closely. I just had so much fun because it was the first time that I've really been able to be at the beginning of a new character. *That* I really enjoyed. I've designed some characters that I hate in commercials and stuff, but this was a new character who was supposed to entertain people, who was supposed to be funny. We hammered it out and it was a great joy for me. I just love to draw him. I don't know if people like him that

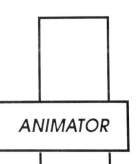

ANIMATOR

much, but I really like him. That's the main thing.

I guess some of the pre-existing characters that I've done that I've enjoyed doing are mainly Popeye. That's because we got to draw him the old way and I love the old comic strip look. So that was a lot of fun working on that. Also, I enjoyed doing Daffy Duck. There was a little tiny sequence in *Quackbusters* that was really fun. We (Greg ford, Terry Lennon and I) were trying to match the old Rod Scribner look from *Prize Pest* for a sequence that was a bridge to the beginning of *Prize Pest* and I was pretty proud of that because I think we managed to come very close to that look: the big slurping tongues and the pin-headed Daffy with the long, tall eyes. We got the McKimson Porky pretty good too. He gets real puzzled and he's straining hard to think and he gets these wrinkly sort of eyebrows on his head. It was a lot of fun to draw. And that was a great joy to do.

I also really enjoyed doing the Maybelline sequence for Ralph [Bakshi] in *Heavy Traffic*. That was a case where I got a lot of design input. The original designer on it was a guy named Bob Dranko, who still works in the business. He did the original boards and then it was my job to take those and essentially make a pose reel out of it. I was under the impression when I was doing it that I was going to animate it later, but Ralph liked the pose reel so much he said, "Don't animate it. Put it in the way it is." I thought, "Oh, no. It'll never play." But a lot of people liked it, because it had a certain liveliness to it. It wasn't real smoothly animated, it was just bursts.

We had a new drawing every six frames, every 12 frames, it went with the beat of the music. It was very stereotyped characters, black characters, and it was very sexy. It was very violent. Something new. Something that I didn't associate with animation up to that time. It was sort of like almost anything you wanted to do. Any of your sexual fantasies or a guy shooting another guy or whatever. You could do anything and we did. And it all worked with the music.

At the time, maybe I didn't enjoy it as much as, say working on Roger or Popeye but in retrospect, I guess you'd have to say it was one of the high points because it was a creative shift. And I was responsible for three minutes worth of film. I had to come up with a lot of ideas for it. Just little bits like his car falls apart. The guy who's driving the car and one door comes off, his window hits his nose, finally the whole thing just falls apart. At one point I remember the car got wet and he had to wring it out like a dishrag. He just picked up the whole car and wrung it out. It was all done with a pose and yet the action read. You could see what he was doing. And that was a great lesson. Sometimes a single drawing can say as much or more than 50 million drawings. You can see it with a single drawing. That was a valuable lesson that I learned from that picture.

Q:
How about characters you didn't enjoy animating, and why?
A:

Maybe, I guess the Fruit Loops toucan would've been one of the characters I least enjoyed doing. He was such a zero, I thought as a character. He's essentially Paul Frees, in the days when he was still alive, doing a very good vocal impression of Ronald Coleman. It's a very cool, sort of laid back character. But he never is a very active character except when somebody's hungry, then he helps them find the Fruit Loops. And he always says the same words in every spot. It's strictly to sell the product. He just didn't have much fascination on his own.

Maybe he was better when they were first starting the campaign, when he was new; when he had his little nephews and stuff with him. I think maybe he was more fun then. But when I was working on it, it was not fun. It was just the same words by rote every time. And very dull. We always had to match a certain look and maybe it's not the way I naturally draw. I'd draw maybe a more bulbous nose, more bigfoot style. It was not enjoyable.

Tony the Tiger was a challenge to do, but not an enjoyable character. The agency has him very set. Who he is, how many heads tall he is, how he's designed, how he acts. He always says the same stuff. Always the same. It's just labor to do something like that because you can't impose anything from your own imagination on him. You just have to take what everybody else does, and match what they've got and then they love it. But if you try and make Tony do a funny walk or maybe twirl his tail a little bit or try and come up with a new little piece of business, that you think helps the spot, they take it out.

Likewise with Snap, Crackle and Pop. They were fun when Vernon Grant designed them in the Thirties. They were really fun little guys with big ears, sort of dwarf-like. Over the years they got more and more blanded out to the point where I can't even look at them anymore. They are not fun for the same reasons I described on Tony and Toucan. You're always taking what somebody else has imagined and trying to duplicate it without adding any of your own to it. I could go on and on, I mean, a lot of commercial characters are that way.

Q:
You probably mentioned these already, but just to re-cap, what project would you say you were most professionally pleased with? And which one did you feel was a failed project?

A:
Let me see. Most pleased with, I guess would be *Roller Coaster Rabbit*. We really rode that one all the way. I had to move to Florida to work on it. I had a little bit of input in the story when I was animating it, because we found a lot of things in the script didn't work or that the boards had to be amplified. I added a whole sequence to it that the director liked. I went through two directorial agendas on it. (They had a change of directors in the middle of the picture.) But it was a great joy to work on because I thought the roller coaster sequence was a lot of fun. It had a great feeling of movement and acceleration and Roger's character was consistent. He was really stupid (chuckle) and he may not have developed any but at least he stayed consistent with who he was. Probably the most fun I've ever had was on that picture. I don't know if anything is going to come as close to that for years to come.

Two projects I'd like to mention are *Sport Goofy* and *Family*

ANIMATOR

Dog (the original *Amazing Stories* episode). Darrell van Citters and *Sport Goofy* helped pull me out of commercials and off a plateau. Darrell really woke me up to a lot of things about timing. Likewise with Brad Bird and *Family Dog* . Both Darrell and Brad are timing masters! They're two of my favorite directors. Other favorites would be Ralph Bakshi, Rob Minkoff and Jerry Rees.

Q:

How about one you feel failed, even if it was a commercial success?

A:

I cover such a wide field, but I guess *Shinbone Alley* might be a good example of something that should, that probably was a good idea but it could've been done so much better. I love the Don Marquis stories, "Archie and Mehitabel," always loved them. I love his free verse. I love a lot of the things that he said. I think a lot of the statements he made in that book were way ahead of his time. He talks about ecology, war, so many things. It's a great book. But they took this little off-Broadway musical, "Shinbone Alley," and some of the songs were not quite right, some of them were redundant, I mean some of the songs were good, but a lot of them should have been taken out. We should have made the picture more like George Herriman style. Because the illustrations in the book were just right. It was a very 1920s look.

They had other designers take it and make it sort of a quasi-Disney-Filmation-ish horror. Just awful. And we had to take and animate that and yet retain a little bit of Herriman's line. When I was cleaning up, I was an assist-ant animator and did a few scenes of animation on the picture, too, we had to take a felt tip pen and do the weighted line; a thick and thin line with a little shading. Everybody put shading on everything in those days. We always had little parallel lines to shade everything and that's the look that we had.

Corny Cole set a lot of the characters for it. Although, I don't think he was the ultimate designer. His designs were watered down by other people too. But I think that's a great example of a failed project. It just died in the theaters. It had to be recut three times, and it's too bad. A lot of young people worked on it, a lot of enthusiastic people, and I loved the material. It's just that we couldn't make it entertaining.

The best sequence in it I thought was the one that came closest to Herriman, which was "Archie Declares War." But it comes out of left field. Here you've got these characters that are more of the Disney style and all of a sudden for no reason at all they change into the Herriman-style characters. It's just to appease whoever was a fan of that style and it stays that way for three minutes and then, pop, it goes back to the other style again. It was a fun sequence to work on, but it ruins the stylistic unity of the picture, and I think it confuses more than helps.

Q:

Would you describe what you feel are the differences of working freelance as an animator versus working in studio?

A:

Sure. The basic difference in freelance is you're self-employed, and you can set your own hours. You are paid with no deductions. You are responsible for all your own taxes, keeping your own records, all your receipts. You have to get a seller's permit and a business license from the city. You have to do all the things that any business would do just to get set up. It's a great education in knowing what the ins and outs of the business are. Record keeping especially is so hard to do. It's just not enjoyable because it's the least interesting aspect of working freelance. But the great thing about freelance is once you get rolling, you can make a living.

It took me nearly a year. (chuckle) I had a pretty hard time when I left Spungbuggy because Spungbuggy resented my leaving. They didn't give me any freelance work and I was hoping that they would. What got me into freelance is that at Spungbuggy I was making barely a hundred and twenty bucks a week for working really hard and working a lot of evenings, weekends and trying to get these spots out. I remember one weekend I was helping a friend of mine do a spot for Spungbuggy. It was a freelance job. And that one weekend I think I made five hundred bucks. I thought, "Oh my God, what am I doing?" I mean (laugh) here I was making more in one weekend than I made in a whole month working for this place on staff. So I said, "Well, I've just got to go freelance." So I gave them appropriate notice and I said I was setting' myself up.

I think the first freelance job I did was on a picture called *The War Between Men and Women* (for Playhouse Pictures), and we were matching the Thurber style. I had a lot of fun working on that. A lot of my stuff got cut out just because directorially they thought some of the animation had to be substituted for with live action. It was a directorial decision. But after that one job I hit a dry spell. I couldn't get work anywhere. And then Duck Soup was starting up. So I picked up some work from them. And then I started to branch out and picked up anywhere and everywhere that I could, mostly in commercials and a little feature work here and there. That's what got me started doing freelance.

I think the big advantage of working in-house over freelance is that you're concentrating hard to do one project or you're always working with the same people all the time. Which is great because you can't get away from it. Whether you're freelance or on staff, film is a collaborative art, especially animation. There is always somebody working with you whether you like it or not. And I think it's better if you know the people you're working with. It's the great advantage of working in-house. You feel more like everybody's pulling together. More of a unified feeling.

Sometimes it gets kind of lonely being a freelancer. And I think you can hit a plateau when you're freelancing. I think I grew for a while and met a lot of people who had a lot of experience but eventually in my animation I felt I was not developing any more. I had come to the limits of what I could do in that system. So the studio system's been helpful for me because it's made me focus more on the communication aspect of what I'm doing. Like, if something doesn't work in the story, speak up. If it's gotta be changed, it's gotta be changed because otherwise it's just going to die like a dog.

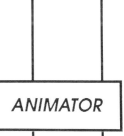

ANIMATOR

I've worked on so many projects where nobody bothered to analyze the story. Nobody cared. They just took whatever they were given and animated it. And that's not your job. Your job is to try and entertain people or sell them something or whatever you're supposed to do. It's communication. I think that's the big advantage of working within a studio system is that it makes you focus more on what your real job is.

Freelancing sometimes you're too concerned with how much money am I going to make this month? I got to hustle here. You're working a lot of nights and weekends. I used to work like four weekends out of five, most of the time, I did that for years and years. I don't know how I did it (chuckle) now I'm getting so lazy. I enjoy being off nights and weekends. I think it's important, too, like what I said before. Because your time off is as important as your time on. So I think that's the basic difference.

Q:

Finally, if you were to advise someone to get into the industry today, how would you tell them to prepare for animation?

A:

Hopefully I'd tell them to do it differently than I did. I think I would tell them to not just study art. I think the study of art is important, especially just good basic drawing, knowing how to draw anything. If you get a teapot, or a locomotive, or a person, or a dog, fat man, thin man, beautiful woman, an ugly woman, whatever, you have to be able to draw it. Just good basic drawing. Learning how to do it.

But along with that, study writers. Study not only good screenplays but, good novels, good non-fiction books, good biographies. I would say get exposed to a lot of ideas through writing. Writing, I think along with drawing, is the heart of animation and how you interpret one and the other. Maybe a good exercise is to take a paragraph or a poem or something from your favorite book and try to animate that. Try to interpret it. Just make it as a piece of entertainment, because that's what you're always running up against over and over again.

Take somebody's vision who may not know a thing about animation. Then you say, "This is a good idea, I can run with this. I know how to interpret it." Then I think that's what makes for a good animator. That's the best possible training, because it all comes down to communication.

I would say study. Get a journalism degree with a minor in art. I think in journalism you're forced to write in a clear succinct way. You learn newspaper style. It's a good clear way to write and I think that's good training. That might be a short cut rather than trying to get a degree in English lit, or something like that. Maybe a journalism degree is more practical because you're really learning just the nuts and bolts of good basic writing. That's what I would advise anybody who wants to be an animator, because being an animator is so many things. I mean, you can study acting, you can study theater design, you can study old movies, whatever it takes, it's all part of it. But I think the basic thing is drawing and writing. That's the two basic skills.

*Photocopy of
animation rough of Goofy in MICKEY'S
PRINCE AND THE PAUPER*

© Walt Disney Company

ANIMATOR

Glen Keane, in less than a decade, has risen to be one of the Disney studio's most prominent animators. Achieving early critical notice for his dramatic bear fight in The Fox and the Hound and his comic characterization of Willie the Giant in Mickey's Christmas Carol, Keane has become a highly visible proponent of the Disney school of animation. His latest work includes Ariel in The Little Mermaid. Keane lectures regularly on the art of animation and has even taught classes at Cal Arts, his alma mater. We found Keane in one of his unusual "down times" between pictures at one of Disney's Glendale animation facilities. As we talked, we took time out to watch a buffalo head being hung in his office, which he shares with Geefwee Boe Doe, an assistant.

Glen Keane

DATE: AUGUST 22, 1990

Q:
Please give a brief description of your career, including studios that you've worked at and specific productions you've worked on.
A:
Well, actually I never really planned to be in animation. It was something that just sort of happened by accident to me. I wanted to go into painting or illustrating. I just knew that I wanted to draw. I didn't know anything about animation. My portfolio went to California Institute of the Arts to get into their school of painting and somehow or another it got sent to the School of Animation and I was accepted into that. I thought, "Oh well, I'll give that a try."

And then I found out about animation. It was a combination of all the arts together. And there was always this sort of ham side of me that wanted to act and I found out that animation was really answering that desire. I love to draw figures, and realized that animation requires a good understanding of anatomy, figure drawing, and I could use all of that information in animation, plus acting.

I worked for a summer at Filmation where I thought that I learned animation. The next summer I came with my portfolio to Disney to show them what I had learned about (chuckling) animation at Filmation. Eric Larson [one of Disney's nine old men] looked through the portfolio. He paged through all the stuff really quickly; all the animation drawings that I'd labored over. He then said there was really nothing

120

there except one little scribbly sketch that he liked. It had some motion and life to it.

He said, "Do more of this kind of thing and just basically forget all the stuff that you thought you knew when you were at Filmation. We don't really look at that as a benefit for coming here to Disney. We want you to really come in with a clean slate where we can teach you."

So I just sort of stepped back and went to the beach and did a lot of quick sketch drawings. I brought them in and they liked them. I started on a two-month training period with other guys at the studio, Ron Clements and Andy Gaskill and John Pomeroy. We just sort of tried to soak in everything that they wanted to teach us. That was in 1974 when I started. It was on the film *The*

Rescuers. Now we've just finished the sequel, *The Rescuers Down Under*. Sort of gone full circle for me.

Actually, I've never thought of myself, really, as an animator. I have always thought of myself as an artist who will animate just as long as it challenges me artistically. And whenever it stops really challenging me then I would leave animation.

I've also done some commercial animation. My favorite was working for Bob Kurtz on a "Burger 'n Bones" dog food commercial.

Q:
You've worked on all the Disney features between *The Rescuers* and *Rescuers Down Under*?

Finished animation rough of THE LITTLE MERMAID's Ariel from "Part of Your World" song sequence

© Walt Disney Company

121

A:

Just about. I can say I worked on all of them but I can't say that all my work is on the screen. I did work in *The Small One* that never got to the screen. I did work in *The Black Cauldron* that never got to the screen, but then so did Tim Burton, John Musker and others. It was like two different pictures that we were approaching.

A:

Well let's see, in *Rescuers*, the first scene I did was Bernard and then I animated Penny mostly with Ollie Johnson. Then after that I guess we went on and did Elliott in *Pete's Dragon* and then it was *The Fox and the Hound*. I did Todd and Vixie and the bear and the badger. From that I went and worked on *Cauldron* . Nothing I did got in the picture. Next I did *Mickey's Christmas Carol* where I animated the giant plus some Scrooge and Mickey.

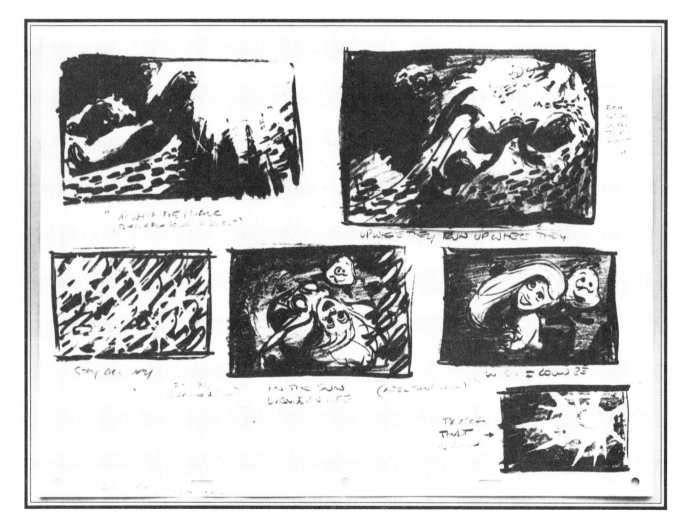

Q:

Can you name some of the characters you did animate in some of the features?

Then I did a little computer test, *Where the Wild Things Are.* We animated a section to Maurice Sendak's book with Magi, the people who had done the computer graphics in *Tron*. It combined computer-generated backgrounds with hand-drawn animation. I did that with John Lassiter. And then after that went on and did *The Great Mouse Detective*. Worked on Ratigan, and did some Basil.

Actually I had left the studio at that time. During *Great Mouse* I worked freelance for Disney at home. Then after *Great Mouse* there was a lull in production so I went over to Chipmunks and did some work with Ross Bagdasarian on *The Chipmunk Adventure*. Did "The Girls of Rock 'n Roll" section in that and then I came back [to Disney] onto *Oliver and Company* and worked on Fagan and Sykes and Georgette on the Georgette song ["Perfect Isn't Easy"].

After *Oliver* was *Mermaid*, which is why I came back. I worked on Ariel in that picture and some of Eric. That, to me, was a challenge because they had originally asked me to do Ursula, the villain. I felt like "No, I want to do something different." I needed a challenge and wanted to do something more subtle and Ariel was what really attracted me. After that I started working on *Beauty and the Beast*, going to London and working with a director there. We ended up not going in that direction so I came back to work on *Rescuers Down Under* where I animated this gigantic eagle, Marihoute, with a kid named Cody riding on her back. I just finished that and am starting on *Beauty and the Beast*, designing Beast and animating him.

Q:
What does an animator do?
A:
Let's see, what does an an-

imator do? (Pause) There's so many different ways one can approach that question. Primarily I guess an animator's job in a film is he's the actor. I mean, it just really comes down to, a film is a story and the animator, he's one of the characters in it. He crawls inside to the brain and the personality of that character. He is that character on the screen. Not unlike regular actors.

The only difference is that an actor in theater, TV or in movies gets to use his own body; his hands and expressions. The animator feels those things but the audience doesn't look at him. They look at his drawing, so it's a matter of how well can you draw how you feel? That's really the gift of an animator, is taking his feelings and putting it through his hand and being able to project himself onto the paper.

I guess the challenge that an animator has is to mentally get past the point where he's drawing. He's no longer drawing on the paper. It's not an act of drawing. It's more of a crawling into that page and living in that space that is now a three-dimensional world. So then you can start to draw a character walking away in space and you're not thinking so much of perspectives and all those technical things. Instead you're thinking, how does it feel? How do I feel walking down this meadow and back behind that tree back there and then sliding along the trunk of the tree and resting, looking up at the leaves? How do I feel? Hopefully you get into it, otherwise the animation has a very technical and studied look and it doesn't ring true. But an animator that can really live in the character that he's drawing, his stuff sparks with life. People believe him.

Storyboard os song sequence "Part of Your World" from THE LITTLE MERMAID

© Walt Disney Company

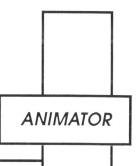

ANIMATOR

Finished rough of Fagin from OLIVER AND COMPANY

© Walt Disney Company

Q:

Can you give an example of films that showcase good animation and possibly bad animation?

A:

Can I do it tactfully? That's another question. For one thing I feel that there should be another term used for Saturday morning animation, the kind that you see on TV. It's a whole different thing. It's more formula. These sort of expressions we plug in at this time in the story and it's a formula story told and it's formula drawings and it's not a personal experience of an animator living in that character. I don't consider that the same as what I do. There's different limitations to that and I think it's almost unfair to criticize them too harshly for the restraints that they're under.

I think that as we got into some of the later animated features in the Seventies at Disney, I didn't feel that the animation was being pushed out to new fronts. It was becoming very formularized. They knew how to do certain things and they did it well. They stuck to that.

I think of *The Little Mermaid* and Duncan Marjorybank's animation of Sebastian [the crab]. Here's a guy that his own expressions and his own personality came out in that character. You could ask Duncan to make an expression on his own face and you saw it was the exact same thing that the crab was doing. I mean, his whole way of thinking was translating from his head through his hand and into that character. The timing, his thought, everything, he transferred into that character. I thought that the character was completely Duncan. You get another animator and the character would've been com-

pletely different. There was no formula to it, and that's a good sign.

The best thing about Disney animation, I feel, is that we try to encourage animators to be themselves in their animation. Sometimes in other animated features, there's a formularized look and each character almost acts the same. You can plug any animator into animating that character, and they're gonna look the same. It shouldn't work that way. Each animator should come up with something completely new, different and personal.

Q:

How do you approach animating a new character when you start?

A:

You get done with one feature and you're getting started on a new one and there's sort of a lull. That's exactly what's happening here now. Just trying to relax a little bit from the last picture where you're running a hundred miles an hour trying to get the thing done. Suddenly, now you've got all this time. I take advantage of it to just be free and not let myself get under too much pressure to perform.

My job is now to design the Beast for *Beauty and the Beast*. This is my time for allowing myself to just get inspired. I'll look at films, and go to places where I think that I might get inspired. Like we're going to go to the zoo tomorrow just to draw. So we have this buffalo head and this thing [a wild boar's head] up in here. Hopefully something's going to rub off. And I put pictures around myself, or read different things. I'm just allowing myself any input from any direction. Giving myself as much of a chance as possible to come up with something new and different.

I know I could sit down if I had to and design a Beast. I could do that and it would be fine. It would work and it would animate, but I keep wondering well, am I cheating the audience somehow? Eric Larson was always saying that to me. When I was animating something and he was going over it with me he'd say, "You know, I think you're cheating the audience here," meaning you could've done more. An animator should never cheat the audience. You're the only one that knows that you didn't do everything you could've with it and the audience doesn't know that

they've been cheated. I just want to make sure I'm not cheating anybody by taking an easy out.

So I'm looking at a lot of art and getting inspiration from as many angles as possible. It's my

first step. Then once I surround myself with that I'll start to draw. I'll come up with some designs and at first the designs are usually very complex and overly analyzed and worked out and they're not too animatable. Then I start moving it around a little bit and the shapes become simpler just because when you constantly have to draw something over and over and over again you're naturally going to come up with a simpler way of drawing a complex shape, unless you're

ANIMATOR

insane and you like pencil mileage that much. So just through that process it simplifies itself.

You try to get a voice to a character that's going to inspire you, too. And that has a lot to do with it. Once you match the voice with the design it may change the design quite a bit. Like with Ratigan in *The Great Mouse Detective*. Ratigan was a very skinny little character. He was a rat and we had him kind of as a weasly-looking guy. But in design he was too similar to Basil. I was thinking maybe we should be really bigger with him.

At that time we were also looking at a film with Vincent Price. It was *Champagne for Caesar* and listening to his [Vincent's] dialogue, I realized that's the voice for me. He just had this sharp, quick way of speaking and the timing was great. You could tell he enjoyed being a rotten guy. And like Ratigan, he also felt like he was justified in doing whatever he did. Like he was unjustly treated, which is important for a villain. The villain isn't bad just because he's bad, but he's justified. He feels like he's right. I started doing drawings based on that with a much larger, huge rat character and it fit. So then we started heading in that direction; we brought Vincent Price in.

With Ariel, the little mermaid, I started surrounding myself with pictures of different girls who were about that right age. Teen magazines and then also Sherry Stoner, who was doing the live action reference for Ariel and, a picture of my own wife who I had been drawing ever since we've been married. It's really natural to draw her. And all these things just sort of came together to come up with a design that was Ariel. I worked closely with Mark Henn and Philo Barnhart in zeroing in on the final design.

Q:
On an average daily routine what do you do in the studio?
A:

Okay, let's go past the point where we've already done our design and we've gotten our layouts and are going ahead and animating. I get in about nine o'clock in the morning and get a cup of coffee and sit down and usually, at the beginning of the week, figure out what it is that I want to get done. I'll take a scene and think it should take about a day and a half to animate this scene. I know that by the end of that day and a half or that second day I'd better be done with this thing.

Usually at that time that's when the telephone rings and there's some meeting that's called. That goes to about 10 o'clock, then at 10 o'clock I decide I better get to work and start to draw and then there's a knock at the door. It's a trainee who wants to show me their work. So I go over their work. And then we have lunch. Then around one o'clock I better get working and I spend about 15 minutes and the directors call. There's a meeting over the layouts. About three o'clock I get to start drawing on the scene and then it gets to be 5:30, 6:00 and I have a decision to make. Is my family more important than my animation? So I leave to go home.

I come back the next day and I know this is the day I said I was going to have my scene done. Same thing starts off. Finally I just skip lunch and I stay in. I know I can get a good unbroken hour of work in at lunch time. I animate through the thing as fast as I possibly can. I use a fat, thick pencil and this actually works out well because the speed that I feel like I'm forced to animate makes me not become overly analytical in my work. I just sort of dive into it and draw it as fast as I can.

I try not to get caught up in the details. I dash through the scene and rough it out in what I call a scribble test. If I can just get it scribbled, by that deadline I've given myself, then I'll feel good. It's really just getting it moving. And any one of those drawings may look terrible to somebody else; to me they look nice because they capture the feeling that I'm looking for. An audience would not necessarily relate to those drawings much but in motion on the screen you get an acting scene across.

I shoot it and I'll show it to the directors, and get their input on it. Usually they feel pretty good about it, and I'll send it out and go on to my next scene for the next day and try to do the same thing and the same cycle goes over again. Get a couple scenes animated in a week or a long scene, whatever. Then after that, eventually, I've got to go back into those really quick little scribbles and tie them down into something my assistants can follow to do the inbetweens and the clean up.

I've got to make it very decisive. What exactly do I want those eyes to be doing there? I can't just scribble it like this, I've got to make it more clear. What I like to do, if I'm working on a sequence where there's a whole lot of scenes, is try to rough through as much of it as I possibly can. Scribble 'em all down so I can tell the continuity and the acting in the scenes. Then we can judge it by stepping back and see if it's all working together as a whole rather than getting caught up in one little tiny part of it and spending all my energy on a three-foot scene when there's 200 feet to do around it. And then we can make some changes on if it's too slow at this point or too fast, and go back and adjust it. Anyway, that's kind of my approach.

Q:

How much freedom are you usually given on a production, as an animator?

A:

I guess it depends on how confident the director is on the sequence that you're working on. If the director feels really confident that this is just what he wants then you're not given that much freedom, which isn't necessarily a bad thing because instead of freedom you're given direction. In other cases the director doesn't really know exactly what he wants. You're given a lot of freedom but, that means sometimes you're not given much direction either. And you're required to come up with that yourself. Most of the time for me personally, I get a lot of freedom on what I do.

I'll often storyboard it myself. Something will have already been storyboarded, but I'll look at it and I'll listen to the soundtrack and think "Gee, what if we did it this way" or "maybe we're missing something here." I'll run it past the directors and they'll agree or they'll disagree. If they say "no," I'll go with it the way it's boarded and approach it that way. If they agree with what I'm saying then I'll go through and I'll board it out and take it from there and start working with the layout guys. It all depends.

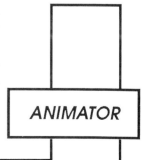

ANIMATOR

Q:

What has been one of your favorite characters to animate, and why?

A:

Usually the last character that I just animated has always been my favorite one. I've always felt that way on everything I've worked on. But if I step back a little bit and look at it, each character has got a unique thing. The eagle, in *Rescuers Down Under* has taught me that real life is as entertaining as anything that I can think of in my imagination. Capturing how an eagle flies is really rewarding if you can make it feel real. Ariel is really rewarding in that I got to capture subtle expressions and feelings on her. I'd have to say that is what I liked the most about her. Ratigan, I just loved to hate that guy. He's such a jerk, and so much personality that it kind of screamed to come out. A villain, to me, always has this power that's just demanding to come out and you want to animate it out of there. And the bear in *The Fox and the Hound*. There's this fierce rage that you wanted to animate. I couldn't draw it big enough, mean enough. Willie the Giant, in *Mickey's Christmas Carol*, to me, was my son, an 18-month-old baby with a big giant body that I really enjoyed doing. Just this real naive, innocent big guy. My favorite, I don't know.

Q:

Have you had a character that you did not really enjoy animating?

A:

Well, I guess Elliot the dragon, in *Pete's Dragon*. I never really got into him as a character. Fagan. I enjoyed him but I always had a basic disagreement with the approach on design. I wanted him to be a short, fat little guy and instead he was a tall, skinny guy. I enjoyed animating him but I don't think I ever got into that character as much as I would've liked to, not that I didn't try. Eric in *Mermaid*. I would've liked him to have more depth of character. Instead he was kind of a standard prince. I wanted to do more with him. But the decision was made that you don't want to start building the story around Eric; the story was really Ariel's. It's difficult to come up with somebody really interesting and unique when you don't want to expand that character.

Q:

Which project do you feel most proud to have been associated with?

A:

Well, it's probably *Little Mermaid*. I think that was because it was the first time that I thought we were doing a project that we were potentially breaking through the barrier where we had just never gotten past before. It was the first picture I think we got the monkey off of our back; the stigma of trying to live up to a tradition. We really broke out into something of our own.

Q:

Is there a film that you've worked on that you weren't really pleased with the final results. Even though it may have been successful, you personally felt it didn't live up to expectations?

A:

Each film will fall short of its potential to one degree or another. I've got to focus on my part of that picture. Did I do my best? Even if a picture turns out to be a dog, if I did my best, I can still feel proud.

Q:

If you were to be starting today trying to become an animator, what do you think you would need to do?

A:

Well, if I was just starting as an animator I would take drawing really seriously. A lot more seriously than probably a lot of other animators would say, but that's me; that's how I approach it. I guess there's different schools to animation. There's maybe a school that says if you just animate very simple shapes then it's more the acting involved and you don't need to get involved in the anatomy. To me, I feel like if you're going to really push into where I think acting needs to go, and we're going to really compete with live action, then our acting needs to go to levels where you're really dealing with subtle, deeper human emotions. The only way you can really capture that, besides being in touch with your own heart in your acting, is to be able to draw how you feel. It requires a real understanding of anatomy and to be able to draw really well, to communicate.

So I would draw and draw and draw as much as I can the people around me, capturing attitudes, look for the subtle things that interest you and draw those. The way a little girl sits with the legs crossed is really entertaining. It doesn't need to be a gag or a joke, it's just looking for those real things, developing an eye for observation. Seeing it and being able to draw it. Get a lot of sketch books. Do quick sketch trying to capture action. Study live action films. I'd say learn the techniques that the old animators did but don't approach it as a formula. Don't get fooled into thinking this is the way to do a walk; this is the way to do a run, a take. Study and discover a new way.

I remember we were up at Cal Arts one time when somebody asked me, how many different takes are there in animation? And I was thinking, "how many different takes are there?" I stopped and said, "where is this question coming from?" I mean, how many different takes *are* there? "What is a take," I asked? The student said, "I don't know? what do you mean?" I answered, "What *is* a take? It's just an animation term. We assume it means something, but what does it mean?"

A take is a reaction. As many emotions as there are in human nature, that's as many takes as you can have, and how each person is, they're going to react a little different. There is no limit to the number of takes. You just need to analyze it. Get into that unique character and animate that.

Animation people, especially students, are constantly trying to compartmentalize it and break it down into "there are this many approaches to doing things." That is very limiting. We have a world of life to discover. Every person and living thing is unique. An animator needs to see that uniqueness and reflect it back to the audience in his work.

ANIMATOR

John Pomeroy is one of the top draftsmen in the animation field today. His control of the pencil is well known within the industry, as is his speed. John's work is much in evidence in the features produced with his two associates, Don Bluth and Gary Goldman. A fan of both classical Disney animation and the broad caricatures of Chuck Jones, John blends the two into a striking style of his own. We talked with John at his office in the Sullivan Bluth U.S. Division studio. There he oversees a small staff of artists who not only contribute to the various Sullivan Bluth features, but also handle a number of smaller, less publicized, projects.

John Pomeroy

DATE: AUGUST 21, 1990

A:
Could you please give a brief description of your career in animation, including studios you've worked for and specific productions you've worked on?

Q:
My first encounter with a professional animation studio was at age 14. I took a portfolio of my work to the Disney Studios. They had no training program and they were not hiring any new artists. However, the guard at the gate really liked my work.

I was discouraged, but just the fact that I got to step on the very ground where the animation mecca of the world was, prompted me to continue in trying to get a job there. My whole being was concentrated on getting a job in

the animation department there. Funny, what I wanted to do and what I ended up doing were two different things.

I wanted to be background painter. I painted portraits and landscapes and still lifes, and anything else to earn the money to go to art school. Finally, after three portfolios and three failures, I was accepted. Feb. 7, 1973, was my first day and I was almost hyperventilating with excitement. I had earned my way.

That same day, I met Gary Goldman, my partner. He came sniffing around, looking at my drawings, giving me encouragement, and a slap on the back. He was my first friend at the studio. It was an interesting period. I wanted to paint backgrounds. They said, "You'll become a better background artist if you work

in animation for a while, get your feet wet, and then you can learn how to paint backgrounds for animated movies. The painted background can't be a piece of art on its own. It must yield and glorify the animation, not dominate it." I agreed and said, "Okay, I'll give it a shot."

I created my first personal test, which was a little stupid animated frog with a little assistant turtle. He had a magical hat which grows so large that it eats the frog. It was awful. But when I saw the first pencil test and the frames going by of the graphic drawings that I had created, and the movement...something that I had drawn was actually moving. It was like no thrill I had ever had in all my artistic life. I threw away the paint brushes and I decided I was going to become an

animator. I haven't painted since. That was 18 years ago.

I think it was the right choice, because, on an esthetic level, I get no thrill greater than to create something from nothing on paper. I was put under the supervision of Frank Thomas, who was one of the "nine old men." I worked with him on 120 feet of running continuity at the end of *Winnie the Pooh and Tigger Too* when they tell Tigger he can't bounce anymore. They gave me a sequence with pathos! I couldn't believe that they would give me, a fledgling rookie, a sequence with that kind of acting in it.

It was then that I experienced one of my most frustrating initiations into animation. I was animating a walk of Tigger going away from the audience very sadly in the snow. The scene was

Charlie model sheet from ALL DOGS GO TO HEAVEN; based on drawings by Don Bluth and Pomeroy and cleaned up by Pomeroy

© Goldcrest & Sullivan Bluth Ltd.

going to be used three times, so Frank wanted to make sure it was right. He had me re-animate that walk 17 times. It was excruciating. By the eighth try, you burn out on the scene. By the 12th try, you're ready to go look for work elsewhere. But, no matter how many times I was down and discouraged, there seemed to be some little flicker of hope that the next attempt at the walk would make it that much better.

It was all worthwhile once I saw the pencil test on the screen. There was a small impromptu audience in one of the screening rooms, and they were actually either crying or laughing. When Tigger walked away in the snow, I could hear some of the audience sniffing. It's that moment that makes the animator so delighted with that which he creates that it keeps him going. An animator may be involved with an animation project for a year, maybe five years, but after that, he gets to sit in the theater and watch his work being appreciated by the audience.

Animation does it better than live-action, for some reason. The memory is fixed and it stays with you longer, from childhood all the way up to old age. It's fixed. It's like your own dreams have come to reality. It's hard for live action to compete with that. After Winnie the Pooh, I worked on *The Rescuers.*

I started hearing small bits of complimentary dialogue. "Did you see that walk?" "That looked terrific." "Did you see John's scene?" It was a high point in my career to be able to hear about your work and how it's appreciated by your mentors and your colleagues. It was a wonderful honor. Again, it prompts you into doing the extra bit of work

that may be needed on a scene. If you feel that the scene isn't turning out the way you want, it's worth the extra investment of time to sweat and make that scene work, because it'll be that much more entertaining on the screen.

After *Rescuers,* I worked as a directing animator on *Pete's Dragon* along with Don Bluth and Gary Goldman. It was a combination of live action and animation. That was a challenge in itself. After that, I became directing animator on *The Small One,* a Christmas featurette. *The Fox and the Hound* was next.

It was a time when I wasn't very happy with the creative direction in which the studio was going. My enthusiasm for working at the Disney Studios had faded because, one, Walt was not there, and, two, the regime that had taken over, wasn't listening to the needs of the artists. There was a lineup of stories and features that they were getting ready for production. None of them really excited me.

So Don and Gary and I started to prepare to leave. We knew we would be leaving, but we didn't know when or where. It all depended on something we were developing on the outside called *Banjo the Woodpile Cat,* a little 30-minute animated TV featurette that we had been working on for three years. It started out to be a training film for us to increase our knowledge of the production of animation. Then it turned out to be our exodus film. We were able to raise money based on it for a feature film that we would produce on our own, independently, as a company.

In mid-September of 1979, we did receive financial backing for the feature *The Secret of Nimh,* and we left Sept. 13, 1979. Once we finished *Banjo*, we began to work on *The Secret of Nimh,* which took us almost two years to produce. It was released in the summer of 1982. We had poured our hearts out into that picture. After two years of work, we were disappointed because it never really went into full release.

I don't think *The Secret of Nimh* was ever played in more than 600 theaters. So no one knows how well it could have done had it had a full release in, say, 1,800 theaters. It might have done a lot better than it did. I think it has broken even with cassettes, with foreign release and all other ancillaries. I still hear people commenting on *The Secret of Nimh*. They come up to me and say, "that's one of the best films you've ever done."

We then got involved with arcade games. We produced *Dragon's Lair, Space Ace,* and then a sequel to *Dragon's Lair,* which was called *Time Warp*. The reasons for doing that were financial. We didn't have enough money to sustain ourselves on a feature budget. So this was a way to keep our artists in-house and keep our enthusiasm alive for the art form. The games were very popular. Even today, we are still able to generate some excitement on a commercial level to try to get those games back in circulation again. I'm hopeful that one day we'll be able to produce a *Dragon's Lair* movie.

Following the arcade games, we became involved with Steven Spielberg. He wanted to meet the people who produced and directed *Nimh* because he thought that style of art form, that type of intricacy and attention to detail and effects had disappeared from the face of the earth. Our meeting

went very well. We sat there for about two-and-a-half hours and just talked about animation. He wanted to find a story that he thought would be worthy. A couple years after the games, he found a property that was called *An American Tail*.

We had an idea that it was going to do well, but we had no idea how incredibly well it was going to do. It earned well over $50 million on its first release, which was beyond anybody's expectations. It was an interesting time because our studio was leaving the U.S. to go to Dublin, Ireland. The week *An American Tail* premiered here in the United States, we were packing and getting ready to go to Dublin. We really couldn't feel the whole impact or the excitement of what was happening here.

I got a little glimmer of it when I went to a Sears department store, where they had a huge exhibit of nothing but Fievel dolls, posters, and objects from the movie. There were kids and mothers and tons of people who were buying these dolls and T-shirts and pajamas and pillow cases. I could hear people talking about the movie, about going back and seeing it again, and taking their friends. I was just wowed by all of this. So I had a feeling that we truly had a success.

An American Tail was, I think, the first film that kind of gave animation a kick in the pants. No film had done that kind of box office business. It was breaking all previous animation records. I think it was the beginning of the animation renaissance. It had been a long time since an animated film had gone up there and done that kind of business in competition with all the great live action pictures.

ANIMATOR

After that, we began work in Ireland on our next feature, *The Land Before Time*, which was released in November 1988. It, too, was very successful. Right now, it's hectic because I'm sort of like in the middle of air traffic control. We have one feature taking off called *Rock-A-Doodle*. We are in production on a movie called *A Troll in Central Park*. And, we have three or four other properties lined up on the runway ready for take-off into production. We definitely have our hands full.

Q:

What art schooling have you had?

A:

My formal art education was at the Art Center College of Design. I went there for two semesters. I was trying to get enough work to show an animation studio what I could do. I had planned and I had written letters to the California Institute of the Arts at the point when they were converting over from Chouinard to Cal Arts. What they wrote back was a turn-down of my portfolio simply because it was too real. They wanted more abstract art work in their applications. But I was accepted over at the Art Center. Maybe that was for the best.

Prior to that, I attended Riverside City College, where I was in their art department for about two-and-a-half years. Until then, my only art education was anything that I could do on my own, from age 3 to 18 or 19. I was sculpting. Painting. Making marionettes, string puppets and hand puppets. Carving. Doing everything I could to find out what my best expression of art was. I knew it had something to do with

my hands because I loved to draw and I loved to sculpt. But as far back as I can remember, I always got a thrill out of making inanimate objects move.

I remember seeing *The Time Machine*, H.G. Wells' novel made into a movie. And I went home and I duplicated the inside of a morlock's cave, sculpted the morlocks and moved them around in the setting. My subconscious was telling me something. Even though I liked to draw, something was coming up to surface that I really didn't know how to express, or how to harness, or address it, until I started working with puppets.

I was making a replica of the Pinocchio puppet and needed references. I wanted to make it look just like the puppet that was in the movie, because it had so much charm. I went to the library and told the librarian, "I need a reference on Pinocchio." She gave me a book called *The Art of Walt Disney,* that was written back in 1943 by a man named Robert Fields. He wrote it while they were working on *Fantasia, Bambi* and *Dumbo*.

I became less and less interested in making a marionette, and more and more interested in this book. I read it five times. I started to draw the figures. It was profusely illustrated with many drawings and many photographs. I started drawing Mickey Mouse. I started drawing Donald Duck and the dwarfs. I started finding out what cels were about and painting the backgrounds. I wanted to duplicate a cel set-up. And the way I did this was by taking the wrapper off a loaf of Roman Meal bread, because I didn't have cels. I didn't even know what they were.

I took the wrapper, and with a brush, I outlined a drawing that I had done in paint. I then painted it on the same side, and put it against the painted background and framed it. (Laughs) I had no idea what I was doing, but all of these feelings were now really coming up to the surface strongly, and they were telling me animation. Go into animation.

Q:

How did you finally break in?

A:

I thought perhaps if I wrote letters to the Disney Studio, they would encourage me and give me information as to how I could get admittance. So I started writing letters to the supervisor there in 1964. Later when I was finally working there, they showed me a two-foot stack of letters they had saved from this nut named John Pomeroy! I wrote every week. I wrote, "Please tell me about your Xerox processing." "Please tell me about what type of cardboard you do your illustrations and background art on." "Please tell me what kind of watercolor paint you use." "Please tell me which library and where I can get good books on animation."

I got lots of letters. One particular letter said, "Please, do not write us anymore unless you have something intelligent to ask us." The letters I got most often all say the same thing, "Thank you for your interest that prompted you into writing us. However, we are fully staffed for the 1965-66," onward, "years. However, it is encouraging to note that you are interested in animation. Best of luck." Blah-blah-blah. But I continued.

I had done some personal tests up to that point. If you look at my first test, it would be encour-aging to anybody young or old who was just entering animation. My first test was horrible. As a matter of fact, I have it right up there [indicates a shelf]. It's in that little plastic bag. I keep it here to keep me humble. If I get too outrageously critical with any of the trainee animators with whom I'm working, I can always pull that out and look at where I was.

Q:

What does an animator do?

A:

An animator brings life to an otherwise still or lifeless object. However, the object that he's bringing life to is all inside his head. He has to imagine a living, breathing personality, what it's going to do or how it's going to act, how it's going to move and entertain. And then realize that thought, analyze it and duplicate it graphically on paper in drawings that give you the illusion of movement. That's the rudimentary analytical explanation. Every animator has his or her own style or approach. It's like every actor who goes on stage; they all have their own little insights, their own little tools, their own little secrets that they usually don't share with anybody else, unless they have a protege.

What I do is get inside my head and imagine I'm seeing a screen. I'm imagining myself in a theater. Let's take a scene from the past on *Nimh*. I had an assignment with a character called the Great Owl. I had never animated an owl. I had never animated a bird in my life. Certainly, I had never animated anything so dignified as the voice of John Carradine, who voiced the owl. So what I had to do was visualize it in my head and then improve

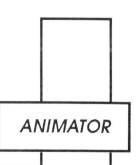

ANIMATOR

the visualization from my head with any good practical references, like live action footage of birds flying, of what it was like recording a voice like John Carradine. He had quite a presence when you were in front of him. You didn't direct him. You simply asked him to do something, and what he gave you was it.

Remembering how he walked onto the stage left an impression on me that gave me the idea of how to animate this owl. It was a particular scene where he says, "It is night. I have to go." He walks out on the end of the limb of the tree, opens his wings, and lifts himself up into the night. John Carradine was wracked and riddled with arthritis. He could barely walk. He held a cigarette in the most impossible way, with his arm and hand scrunched. His bones were fused together. He could barely hold a cigarette and yet he was able to smoke. He walked with a limp in a sort of hunchback fashion.

At first, it was a sad-looking impression. Afterwards, after you put the man together with his physical appearance, suddenly he's very majestic in some strange, supernatural way. I wanted to put all of these qualities in this scene. The mechanical, physical of how he walked, and then trying to analyze that walk. I shot footage of myself mimicking that walk so I could get something that looked authentic, because there is a certain dramatic feeling that you want to put into the paper that you want the audience to feel. Yet, there are the basics of physics that it has to adhere to. It has to have weight. It has to have power. It has to look like there's flesh and bones beneath feathers. It can't move like a mechanical man made out of tin.

All of these intricate little details put flesh and bone into the scene and make it radiate off the screen and make it believable. There's one thing that animators are always thinking of, and that is the suspension of disbelief. In other words, you want the audience to sit before these painted images and forget that they're paint, forget that they're animated, forget that they're created on paper, and accept them as if they are real living beings. That's what I was hoping to do with this character. I put a lot of work into this one scene where he walked out on the limb. Constantly, all the way through the scene, I'm remembering John Carradine. He was a great influence on me animating that scene. The way he held his cigarette and the way he walked is what the Great Owl was.

When you animate a body, when you animate a fish or a cat or a dog or an owl, you want it to be different from anything else you've ever seen. You want to put your signature on the canvas. Yet you don't want people to see the brush strokes. You don't want to remind people that it's drawn. You want to say to them, "this really exists."

Q:
Can you give me an example of a film that has good animation and a film that has bad animation?

A:
Badly animated films I always associate with a lot of the highly commercial types of film. A film that goes out there just to sell candy or books or games or product is a badly animated film.

I've seen one film that I don't much care for. It was a version of the book, *The Last Unicorn.* I don't remember where it was done, but it was badly animated. They were cardboard, cut-out figures that radiated no life, that were flat, undimensional, uninspiring. It was a torture of an animated story to sit through for an hour-and-a-half. That to me represents bad animation; taking all the shortcuts, putting no love into the product, using it as a commercial vehicle to sell merchandise, and not really taking full advantage of the story.

There are so many examples of good animation. One of my favorites is [Disney's] *Peter Pan.* On an aesthetic level, it represents the very best. It represents the best of how they were able to make human characters move and how to make fantasy characters. The quality of the animation was some of their [Disney] finest. It was like they were stepping out of the early era of *Dumbo* and *Pinocchio* and they were entering into the more sophisticated worlds of *Sleeping Beauty* and *Lady and the Tramp.*

At that time they still retained all of their cartoony feelings and their cartoony aspects, of doing stretch and squash and doing impossible things with animation. Yet getting a beauty and a reality that had never existed before, and amalgamating the two feelings together.

One of my favorite animated characters was in the film— Captain Hook. Although he's a villain and he radiates evil, he also has many different levels. He's frightful. He's frightening. He's comedic. He's stupid. He's grand. He's imposing. He's sniveling. He's so many different things. He radiates so many different facets of his personality and they're all done and animat-

ed with extreme exactness. It's one of the characters that I keep referring to and which inspires me to do what I do simply because he's so real. And he reminds me of people whom I know. I don't think I can recall a character that, in animation, expresses moods and feelings as well as he does.

Q:
What do you do as an animator on a day-to-day basis?
A:

Well, if I'm wearing my producer's hat, Monday morning I have to come in and see how the work in progress is moving. Because of my responsibility, the production end, I am given a sum of money and I have to turn that into a product. I have only so much time in which to accomplish that. This means I am engaged in charts, reports, averages, figures, data day-to-day, every kind of report imaginable. Plus making sure that work is always flowing; that everyone has up-to-date information concerning the script, model sheets and dialogue.

It's a huge task. I review the previous week and all the work that had to be done. All footages have to be counted Monday, before noon, so I try to get all footages out and then get everyone started on new footage coming in. It gets pretty hectic.

Then there's the animation hat. After the excitement dies down, maybe late in the evening, about six o'clock, I'll get inspired to animate a scene. Everyone's gone home. The kids are put to bed. And, I decide to go and raid the refrigerator of animation. What I'll do is I'll sit for a moment, for a long time, and try to visualize my scene. Hope-

ANIMATOR

fully, no one will disturb me, because, at least with me, the animation process is very fickle. You have to conceive of a thought before you animate it. You have to think about it and see what you are doing before you can put it down on paper. If someone disturbs that thought process....

It's sort of like being a pearl diver. Imagine yourself diving off the edge of the boat going down 100 feet to look for a pearl. While you're looking for one, someone wants you to come up to answer a question. They tug on your air line. You swim up 100 feet, you take off your helmet and you say yes? "Did you want me to shine your shoes?" "No." Then you put on the helmet, you go back down 100 feet, and you begin the process all over again. You can't remember where you last looked for that pearl, so you have to start all over again, looking constantly. Then somebody else tugs on your air line. You have to do the whole thing over again.

When someone interrupts my thoughts, it takes me about 20 minutes, even a day, to get back into thinking and feeling the impression, or getting the inspiration on how to animate a scene. But once I get that, I close the door, I answer no questions and I go into a time warp. I can look at the clock and it'll be maybe three in the afternoon. The next time I look at it, it may be nine or twelve. Sometimes it'll be two or three in the morning. But, activity happens. I can see the scene and I am hell-bent to get it on paper.

I begin drawing graphic symbols as fast as I can. Throwing drawings out as fast as I can. Replacing them with new ones. And

I'm not even really involved with the drawing. I could care less about what the drawing looks like. What I'm looking for is an impression that I can flip that looks like action, that looks like the life force is on the paper. Once I get that, then I can draw.

You become totally detached in time. You are totally oblivious to everything around you. My memory suffers. I can't remember things. All I'm doing is being in tune to creating this life force. And by the time the late hour rolls around, I'll have a stack of drawings in my hand that I can look at. And, hopefully, it is a living, breathing thing that's entertaining.

Q:
How much freedom are you given on an average production?

A:
Well, you can do just about anything you want to, as long as it's entertaining and sells the idea and advances the story. I tell my animators to, "Challenge me." If I give you an idea and concept of how this should be acted, you don't have to accept it. But I hope that whatever you do will either top or equal the idea I'm giving you.

If you go below that, then I'm going to impose my ideas on you to get that scene finished and get it completed, because I have to work as a producer, too. Once they know the parameters they have to work with, the amount of action, the mood of the scene, the footage and the acting, they can do just about anything they want. They have complete freedom to do whatever it takes to sell that idea. It's up to them.

Q:

What are the favorite characters of yours that you animate? And why?

A:

I love to animate funny people and I really love to animate villains. Villains radiate this inner fire inside that most other characters in a movie don't share or don't have. They're moody, they're awesome, they're fearsome. Yet they're crying inside. They're also frightened. I have two favorite characters, and both of them are in our first feature, *The Secret of Nimh.* I really enjoyed working on the characters, Jenner and the Great Owl.

But, I've had an enjoyment that I never had before. It was on *All Dogs Go to Heaven.* I got a sequence to animate that was recorded live with Dom Deluise and Burt Reynolds. It was a confrontation when they're arguing. It takes place towards the end of the picture. An animator rarely ever gets a dramatic showpiece to do; say six scenes in continuity, maybe a half a minute's worth of running animation that gets executed. That was really a juicy treat. It was probably one of the most tedious yet one of the most enjoyable pieces that I ever got to animate simply because I wanted it to work more than anything I ever wanted to work before.

Drama is a hard thing to put down graphically. Humor is easy. I can pinch my cheeks, I can scratch my face, I can make faces, I can mug, I can do takes. I can do all sorts of great graphic things that have been done before in animation that'll make you laugh. But drama is very, very difficult, because I'm trying to captivate an audience and have them buy into an emotion that they're going to discount right off the bat, because it's animation. You're supposed to make me laugh with animation. I can make you cry, maybe, and I can make you laugh. But to make you feel tension inside because of the situation existing between two companions, two characters that love each other and are in conflict, that is difficult.

I had a great track to work from. Very seldom do we ever get to put two actors in the room together and have them record live, without editing or cutting any tape back, lay it into the tracks, and then animate directly from that. That's rare. You seldom get to do that. But these two actors, Dom Deluise and Burt Reynolds, had worked so many times before, they knew each other's habits and chemistry. And they put the magic into the sound track. So taking that magic off the sound track and putting it in drawing form was an incredible challenge. I can't think of too many other areas where I was as enthused or as excited about animating.

Q:

What was a character you didn't enjoy animating?

A:

I'm glad you asked that. If you would analyze what I said before—villains being my favorite characters—what do you think would be the one character that I would hate to animate? A saint.

One of the most boring assignments I ever got was Don asking me to animate St. Joseph in *The Small One.* St. Joseph was a very, very nice man. But in animation, he was boring. All I could think of was that he radiated goodness and fatherliness. I

ANIMATOR

couldn't understand where he was coming from. I couldn't get into the mode of imagining what he would think or feel. I couldn't get inside of his character. All I did was imagine. I animated a piece of waxwork on wheels that moved around and smiled. It was inane. It was not my favorite assignment.

Q:

What project have you worked on that gave you the most professional satisfaction?

A:

As far as personal satisfaction in regards to aesthetics, me personally as an artist and an animator, I have none I can think of. I've named some characters that I've really enjoyed working on, but as a total tapestry, when I look at all the works that I have done, I don't know which one gave me the most satisfaction. I wish I could.

Maybe that's because it's coming up. I'm enjoying working on our current picture, *Troll in Central Park*, I think because I am thoroughly involved in the story, thoroughly involved in the characters, thoroughly involved in the animation, and probably more involved in different aspects of the picture and the production more so than any other picture I've ever been associated with.

Most of the time in the past, it's just been me and animation. Tunnel vision between me and the paper. This is giving me a chance to sort of spread my wings, so to speak, and get involved with a lot of areas that I've never been involved with. You can get involved with story and become involved with a character design and the animation, the color, everything

through the final work print. I'm getting to see my ideas work on a wider range.

Q:

What advice would you give to someone who wanted to get into the business today?

A:

It's a lot easier now than it was 20 years ago when I was trying to get in. There are more training programs. There are more school programs. There are more colleges that have animation classes. It's a hard thing to pinpoint the areas of artistic experience which one needs. Good drawing is first and foremost. Whether it's through figure drawing or drawing landscapes or whatever. To be able to quickly and convincingly put down your thoughts, graphically, so that they are understood by someone else. It's the language by which we all speak. If you can't draw, then you'll be eternally tongue-tied. You have to be able to draw. Getting drawing experience, that's first.

Stimulating your inside expression, or your inside ability to project entertainment that will cause sadness, happiness, love, tenderness is another thing that has to be developed. I'm trying to get our animators to get used to the idea of attending an acting class. The thought that animators are actors with pencils is not new. It's one that few people in the business understand or appreciate. You have to be able to act, then draw it. You have to be able to conceive the gestures, the words, the expressions and all of the movements that are going to make a performance happen on paper.

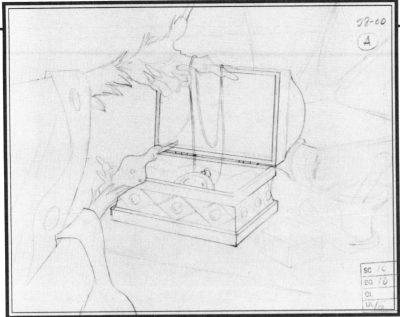

Nicodemus' hands put the magic amulet into its case in *THE SECRET OF NIMH*. Pomeroy used his own hands as models using make-up and false nails

© Mrs. Brisby Ltd.

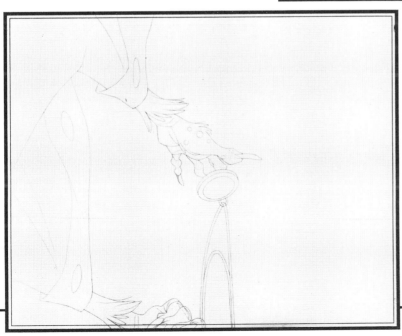

ANIMATOR

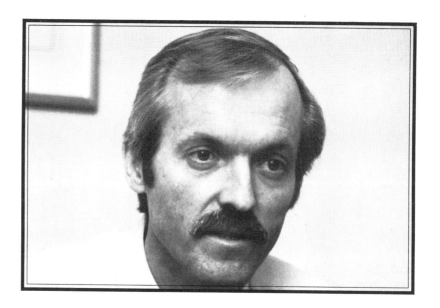

Don Bluth has been one of the most visible animation professionals in decades. While working at Disney in the early Seventies he was frequently singled out as one of the new animation directors likely to lead the studio when the "nine old men" finally retired. Instead he, and a group of followers, left the studio in the late Seventies in a much publicized exodus. His work on the ground breaking DRAGON'S LAIR videogame, a team up with Steven Spielberg in the Eighties, the release of the highly successful AN AMERICAN TAIL and his move to Ireland all made headlines. Today Bluth watches over a gigantic studio in Ireland and a growing annex in Southern California. Still frequently in the spotlight, Bluth's quiet-spoken, eloquent delivery and strong opin-

Don Bluth

DATE: JULY 27, 1990

Q:
Could you please give a brief description, in your own words, of your career in animation?

A:
That's pretty easy. Let's say that my interest in animation goes back as early as when I was four years old. I was very interested in animation, probably because I had seen a Disney picture. The first one I ever saw was SNOW WHITE, and I was very impressed by it. I tried to imitate it way back then by making drawings myself. When I went home I tried to draw the Disney characters and everything else. I went back again and again to see the Disney pictures because I was so attracted to them. And that was, I think, the propellant

that pushed me forward into the business.

I did a lot of drawing on my own. I really never had any formal art training. I didn't like the kind of artwork most of the art teachers I would talk to, or briefly take classes from, taught. It was realistic or it was still life or it was life drawing. I wasn't particularly interested in those things. I was interested in movement and color and entertainment. So, I had no formal artistic training. I just practiced and taught myself how to draw.

I do have a college education, though. I majored in English. I did that because I loved to read and I've always been interested in other people and other countries and other languages. I was a history major, a psych major and a humanities major all rolled into

ions make him a key spokesman for the art of animation.
This interview was done over the phone due to Don's heavy involvement in the final stages of the upcoming post production of ROCK-A-DOODLE planned for an early 1991 release.

Story sketch by Bluth of Timmy from THE SECRET OF NIMH

© *Mrs. Brisby Ltd.*

one. I have since found out that it's served me very well in working with scripts and with storyboards.

I worked for about a year at the Disney studio right out of high school. That was when Walt was at the studio. We worked on SLEEPING BEAUTY. Then I left. Mainly, I think, because I found it kind of boring. I didn't want to do it. I was quite disillusioned.

Then I went away and did many other things. I had a legitimate theatre with my brother, and we did musical comedies in an old Safeway store. After that, I went back to college and later traveled around the world. I finally came back and finished college.

I graduated with an English degree and went back to Cal-

ifornia. I got a job at Filmation doing layouts. It was a good way to pay the rent. I got fairly good at it and was earning excellent money in those days, about 1967. But I wasn't that interested and quickly grew tired. After about three years there I said, "Well, if I'm going to do this for a living, why don't I go back to Disney because they do it right."

So I went back in 1971. It was all very different because Walt was gone. He died in the Sixties. A committee was running the place. The pictures didn't look very good to me. I was now not as encumbered by a romantic film over my eyes. I could see a bit more clearly.

We (my contemporaries and I) tried very hard. We made lots of noise, and worked hard to see if we couldn't make the pictures better, or at least have them measure up to what we had seen in the past when we were children. But, it didn't seem to work. We produced THE RESCUERS and ROBIN HOOD. Some think

quite so hard and brittle. It also occurred to us that maybe, if we went and did this, that Disney would become a competitor and competition is usually what jars people to reality and makes them

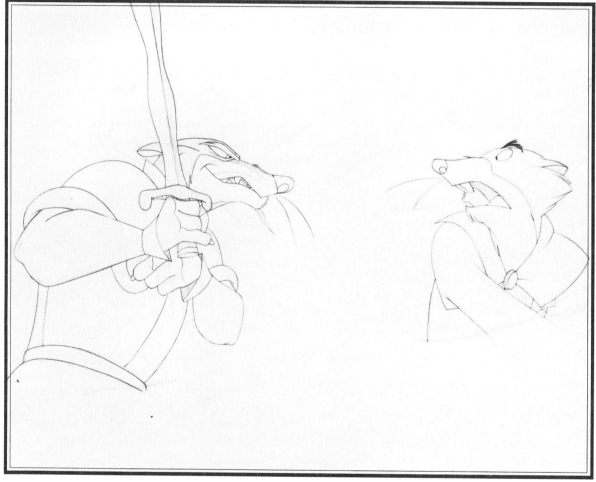

Justin and Jenner in the fight sequence from THE SECRET OF NIMH

© *Mrs. Brisby Ltd.*

they're great pictures but they pale, I think, next to SNOW WHITE, PINOCCHIO, BAMBI and the earlier pictures.

I finally came to the conclusion that it was too late to effect a change at Disney. Their administration didn't want to hear anything. So, on September 13, 1979 (my birthday), John Pomeroy, Gary Goldman and myself and eleven others left the studio, to make our own pictures. We thought that at least we wouldn't be encumbered by a corporate philosophy which was

try harder. So, we needed Disney to try harder just to have that competition.

It was very pompous of us, but we thought that competition would probably wake the sleeping giant. So, we made THE SECRET OF NIMH and indeed, it did cause a few furrowed brows and some other folks said, "Hmmm..." However, THE SECRET OF NIMH was not properly promoted. MGM did not put up any money for prints and ads. We had to raise the money ourselves. It wasn't properly marketed and failed

We thought we were out of business, but along came another opportunity; the arcade games. We went into that business and pioneered the first animation arcade games, DRAGON'S LAIR and SPACE ACE. They were enormously successful. Then the arcade market collapsed and we thought **again** we'd be out of business. When lo and behold, along came Steven Spielberg, who had seen SECRET OF NIMH, and he said, "Maybe you'd like to do a picture with me? I had thought that golden age of animation was over, but SECRET OF NIMH looks like it was made way back when."

We said, "O.K., we'd like to do a picture with you, too." So we began to search for a picture which turned out to be AN AMERICAN TAIL. I think AMERICAN TAIL came along at a very critical time in animation history, because animation was not doing well. I think if Steven had not stepped in and said, "I believe in animation" we'd all probably not be doing too well today.

Disney's last two pictures, THE GREAT MOUSE DETECTIVE and THE BLACK CAULDRON had **not** made money on their first release. Most of the business community said, "Animation has a curse on it. Don't go near it." So there wasn't any money that was readily available for people to make animated films. But he [Steven] convinced Universal to put up nine million dollars to make the movie, AMERICAN TAIL. We made it and everyone said, "Can it make money?"

When AMERICAN TAIL did come out it went out into the marketplace and made fifty mil-

lion domestic, which was a phenomenal return. Steven thought it might make thirty. Then in Europe it made another twenty-five. Then it went to cassettes worldwide and made another, I think, seventy-five million. So we have a take of one hundred and fifty million.

It was promoted beautifully, which also had something to do with the success of the picture. Because that happened, Universal said, "Let's do more." Disney got very excited. The giant was definitely waking up. They did ROGER RABBIT about that time and Steven got involved. ROGER RABBIT was a success. That's two animation pictures in a row that were successful. I think that was the impetus that pushed them in the right direction.

The third picture that came out was THE LAND BEFORE TIME which was extremely successful; more so than AMERICAN TAIL. Disney came out with OLIVER AND COMPANY, and that, too, was successful. That was four pictures in a row that started to work. And about that time everyone in Hollywood said, "Animation works again. Go for it." So companies began to spring up everywhere.

What then happened was that there wasn't enough talent to satisfy the demand. So we began the age of pilfering and bartering and trying to get animators. It was an animators' market. They could name their price, if they were any good. That's still going on today. Of course, the fact remains, **if** the productions which are created during this great gold rush are good productions, I think our business will continue to be healthy. If not? It will take a dive. Most professionals who

DIRECTOR

are in the business know this could happen. We may have seen the beginning of it when we see a picture like THE JETSONS which came out and didn't done as well as was hoped. It did not get very good reviews. So, we'll see what happens.

During the making of LAND BEFORE TIME we couldn't see our way clear to again produce a picture like AMERICAN TAIL for the same price. To do AMERICAN TAIL for nine million dollars we had to freeze everyone's salaries for a year and a half. All of our employees agreed to do it. We could not be members of the [animation] union because the union required the price to be too high and the picture would never have been made.

We froze everyone's salary, and we said, "Let's try this one last time to see if we can get it to work." Well, when it did work, of course, we said, "We can't do this to people anymore, we have to pay them what they deserve to be paid." We told Steven we would not freeze salaries again. So the only thing we could do was to say, "Let's go to a country where we can get cheaper labor and we can pay professional people what they deserve." So we moved our entire studio to Ireland. The people here began to train the Irish people to do what they knew how to do. Also the Irish government gave us tremendous incentives to come here. We got a ten percent tax on our corporation instead of the U.S. fifty percent tax. That allowed the company to make a profit and to grow.

That was the reason we moved to Ireland. The Irish people are very talented and very good workers. It became a haven for us, a good place whose gov-

ernment put its arms around us and began to protect us. Up to that point we had met too much opposition from Disney, from the unions, from whatever was in the marketplace. It was a welcome relief to have somebody actually helping the artists grow. That was good.

That brings us up to date.

Q:

What does a director of animation or animators do?

A:

A director of animation is very similar to a director of live-action. Your job is to see to it that the images and the story that goes onto the screen are produced and executed in such a way that the audience will go through a range of emotions, at the end of which they will be gratified, uplifted, made to feel happy and hopeful about their own lives and to see the world a little differently.

That job is not easily accomplished because the direction of a picture can turn into myriads of tiny little chores and tasks that can eclipse your original purpose. You talk to people daily about drawings. You talk about how to draw a hand, how to draw a foot, how to draw a head. You talk about camera angles. You talk about color. You talk about music. You talk about design **ad infinitum**. All of these things are pieces of the whole. The director must keep these pieces in his head, or at least in a piece of his head, and remember that the objective is to make a composite of all these pieces that spells an emotional experience— and a story. So, a director gets involved in everyone's lives in the studio, their working lives, and helps them to do good jobs so that at the end of it, their picture looks really, really good.

Q:

How much supervision do you feel is necessary, for a director?

A:

Well, you either have to have competent people to whom you delegate work, whom you **know** will come back with the right thing, or you have to go around and supervise everyone at the studio. The writing of the scripts, of course, is most important because without a good script you have nothing. Storyboarding is also important be-

rector and that is **everything** all rolled into one. The storyboarder gives vision to the script. How the drawings are done and what they are saying becomes much more important than whether you can do a good drawing or not.

So, it's very much live-action director thinking. You become very involved with the actor-animators. Those people, actor-animators, are the people who let you know what a character is feeling or thinking or gets you to feel the story itself. You must watch each scene all the way or they may draw hundreds of draw-

Bluth's story sketch of the battle between Justin and Jenner in THE SECRET OF NIMH

© *Mrs. Brisby*

cause that is the cameraman, that is the cinematographer, that is the choreographer and that is the di-

ings and at the end of the day you may say, "That doesn't work at all." If you have to throw them

DIRECTOR

Bluth's story sketch from the opening scene of THE SECRET OF NIMH

© *Mrs. Brisby Ltd.*

all out you throw away a lot of money.

I keep tight control on the color because I think the color is that part of the emotions that you see and feel. So I watch color very carefully and I watch the color models carefully and the painting of the backgrounds. But, when it comes time for many of the service areas, which are getting the picture mechanically true, getting the color tone itself, doing the coloring, marking up the drawing, shooting it, etc. all of that, that doesn't need quite as much supervision. I just leave them alone.

Q:
When does a director of animation usually get involved with a project?

A:
Usually they get involved with a project from its concept. With AMERICAN TAIL it was from the very beginning. We talked about what the story would be and what we wanted the story to do for the audience. We talked about what the mouse was like, what his feelings were like, how old he was, what he felt about his brother, his sisters, what he felt about Mom and Dad, what he felt about coming to America; all of his feelings. Everything was discussed long before we ever made the drawing of the mouse. We tend to consider all of these characters as people, or friends. Then, really all that the mouse is, or the pigeon, or the cats, or whatever, are little masks we put on people. Because animation is a series of masks that are symbols that really stand for us as people.

Q:
What would say is your strongest area in directing animation?

A:
Probably my greatest strength lies in storyboards. I'm still very heavily involved in that. I still draw about six to seven hours a day storyboarding. And, I think the day that I stop doing that I won't be as good a director.

Q:
How much freedom are you usually given on a production as a director?

A:
Complete freedom. I insist on that. If someone else has their hands on mine, I really cannot do the job. It's too hard to explain everything I do to someone who doesn't understand the business. So, I just simply say, "If you want to come in as the Executive Producer and you want to put up the money, then you ought to have confidence that I'll do a good job for you. Don't bother me."

Q:
Now for some personal comments. What film project have you been involved with that gave

you probably the most professional enjoyment or satisfaction and why?

A:

That's a very hard question to answer. I can't really pick one of the children that I like more than the others. I can only say that I've enjoyed every one of them. They've each had a special part of my life and they've each taught me something. It's always very difficult to say goodbye to all the characters when you're not required to draw them anymore.

There's another strange thing I've noticed. I don't understand it. I never go back and look at any of the pictures I've done. I usually see them after the dub and maybe see it during the promotional time. After I've seen the picture with an audience a couple of times I never go back and look at it.

I'm not interested in seeing a picture that's completed. It's kind of painful for me because I've outgrown it. I can see what needs to be fixed. So, I don't go back and look. The challenge for me is the next one we're working on. "How can I make it better?"

Q:

And my last question is: If you were to give someone advice for getting into the business today, how would you say they'd have to prepare themselves?

A:

A good education is really important. Particularly something that has to do with literature, reading, your ability to see through and analyze a good plot, or story; to recognize the poetic expressions; to recognize character relationships since they seem to be the most entertaining.

I would have to say also that the focus of any good director should be to entertain his audience. People must sit in the dark for an hour and a half, two hours, and see something of value that will entertain them but at the same time, perhaps, enlighten them. It may give them a feeling that they are important, that the world is an important place and that it's a great place to live in and a great time to live. Now a director, to do that, has to actually **feel** that. You have to get that from somewhere in yourself. So I would say education, which is the key to all enlightenment. Read, go to college, get a good degree, probably in literature, which means the humanities. Then the next thing to do is: Learn to draw.

I don't think you can be a good animation director unless you have first been an animator. So I would definitely say, "Learn to draw." Your drawings should be as natural to you as thinking. It should not be a conscious effort. You should draw until ten thousand or a hundred thousand bad drawings are out of your system and you can do it as easily as you breathe. Then you can concentrate on **what** you are saying and not **how** you're saying it.

Then we're into animating. Once you learn to animate, you basically have an understanding of the medium. You know how to draw, you know how to animate, then you concentrate on what you're trying to say. If you can master those few things, I would say that qualifies you to become a director. And, hopefully, you have something to say.

DIRECTOR

Ron Clements

Ron Clements, after a brief stint at Hanna-Barbera, has been a key talent at the Disney studio. Though he's only worked on a few projects since his start in 1973, they have proven to be important ones. After several years in animation and story, he co-directed The Great Mouse Detective (1986), one of Disney's most favorably reviewed films in years. He then went on to co-write and co-direct (with John Musker) The Little Mermaid (1989) which won critical acclaim, two Oscars and became the highest-grossing animated feature in history. We met with Ron in one of the buildings that now house Disney animation in Glendale. Around his office were sketches from his current project, Aladdin, set for a 1992 release.

DATE: JULY 7, 1990

Q:
Could you please give a brief description of your career.
A:
Okay, I'm originally from Sioux City, Iowa. I came out to Los Angeles, it'll be 17 years this September. I don't have very much formal education. I was real interested in animation even while I was in high school and I've drawn since I was a kid. I love the Disney films and was heavily influenced by them. As I graduated from high school, I started to think that animation was a career that would be real interesting.

I didn't know how to approach it. I checked in with different art schools and a lot of the classes seemed like they weren't really geared toward working in the industry. I worked at a TV station in Iowa and I got them interested in doing local animated commercials. During that, I did a 15-minute animated film about Sherlock Holmes that got a certain amount of attention in Iowa. Then, people said I should bring it out to Los Angeles and get in the industry. So I came out to L.A.

I called Disney. Disney said they weren't hiring people at the time. Then I got to see someone at Hanna-Barbera, who saw the film. I was hired at Hanna-Barbera and worked there as an inbetweener, which is the lowest rung of the animation ladder. I took evening classes at Art Center at the same time. I worked at Hanna Barbera for about three months on things like *Speed Buggy* and *Inch High Private Eye*,

then I was laid off because that work was seasonal. So, there was a couple of months where I wasn't working, I was sort of knocking on doors.

Then I found out about the Talent Development Program at Disney, which had just been started up in the last couple of years and wasn't well publicized. In fact, the Personnel Department didn't even know about it. I submitted my portfolio and I was accepted into the program. They had a review board with all the older animators who would look at these portfolios. And if they thought you had potential, you were put on sort of a test period, like a screen test. I was on for four weeks. The idea was for you to do your own personal test. You could animate anything you wanted to within that four weeks

and at the end of that time, the review board would look at your work. And if they liked your test, you'd go another four weeks.

So I did that and I got through the first four weeks and after eight weeks, I was put on permanent salary. So I made it through that and then I was an in-betweener at Disney working on *Winnie the Pooh and Tigger Too*. I also did some assistant work on that. I continued to do personal tests and finally moved into animation. I became a character animator on *The Rescuers* and also animated on *Pete's Dragon*. I was a supervising animator on *The Fox and the Hound*.

Then I moved into the Story Department. I did some story work on *The Black Cauldron*, most of which was not used in the movie, then shifted onto *The*

THE FOX AND THE HOUND

© *Walt Disney Prod.*

151

Basil, THE
GREAT
MOUSE DE-
TECTIVE

© *Walt Disney
Prod.*

Great Mouse Detective, or "Basil of Baker Street", before the title was changed. And I did story work on *Great Mouse* and then moved into direction on it.

While that was going on, I had submitted an idea for *The Little Mermaid*, a two-page treatment that had gone over favorably. Then John Musker, who I worked with on *Great Mouse*, and I made a pitch to let us write a screenplay of *Little Mermaid*, which was one of the first times a screenplay had been written for an animated film. So, we wrote the screenplay for *The Little Mermaid* and then we directed it.

That's pretty much it, 16 years and just a few projects, actually.

Q:

At the Art Center, what sort of art classes did you take?

A:

Life drawing, just drawing classes. And then when I started working in the Talent Development Program, they also had a lot of art classes at Disney in the evenings. And those were mostly different types of life drawing classes, oriented toward quick sketch and just trying to improve your drawing ability.

Q:

What does a director of animation or a director of animators do?

A:

Well, I think it's different at every studio. Also, it's a little different with John Musker and myself because we write as well as direct. For example, with *Mermaid*, we were the first guys on the project and probably the last guys off, and involved in pretty much every aspect of the film. Starting out, once the script was written, we got involved with early visual development, early character designs.

Howard Ashman and Alan Menken came aboard and we worked with them as far as the writing of the songs, then we got involved in the casting process and finding the actors. We directed the actors in their voice recordings. We worked with storyboard artists, involved in getting the film put on storyboards and embellished and plussed and made much more visual. We worked with the layout artists in terms of staging and designing sets. We worked with the animators, directing them somewhat like a live action director might direct a live action actor. And we're involved with the background painting, with the color, all through post-production, with the scoring of the film, and the sound effects.

Throughout it all, we're just trying to keep everything consistent. We had 400 artists working on *Mermaid* at its peak. And it's trying to somehow come out with a consistent product where you're still telling the same story and making the same movie even though so many people are involved. And that's essentially what we do.

Q:

How much supervision do you feel is necessary in handling all the people?

A:

Well, we tend to work pretty loosely. Of course, part of that is, that we're dealing with very talented people and we're not trying to train them as much as trying to keep them on a certain level. So, we don't tend to be very dictatorial. I'd say we tend to be fairly easy going. We encourage ideas, we encourage plussing.

We want people to be involved. We want them to feel like it's their movie. I'd say we're protective of the story and somewhat of an overall vision. We'll try to keep things on track.

For example, working with animators I don't dictate the performance. I'll let the animator come up with that. I'll give him certain parameters to work in like, "This is the point of the scene. This is why it's in the movie," but I don't normally act it out for him, which some directors would do. And we don't draw key poses which I think directors at some other studios would do. The animator goes off and he works out the concept of

the scene with thumbnails, and then we go over those thumbnails.

The way we worked on *Mermaid*, we cast the animators like actors in the sense that we would

have each animator focus on a specific character. And they would tend to get possessive of that character which was good. We really liked it when that would happen. For example, the animator would say, "My character wouldn't do that. He wouldn't act like that." In some sense, the character belongs to the animator much more than it belongs to the director. So, we encouraged that. We just tried to keep it all in line.

DIRECTOR

I'm talking specifically about animation, but in all areas, it would be similar to that. We tend to give people a fair amount of freedom. I'd say my approach is if someone comes up with an idea that I think is better than my idea, I'll naturally want to use their idea. Even if they come up with an idea that I think is comparable to my idea, like it's not better, but it's not worse, I'll still want to go with their idea because I feel like they'll be more involved that way. The only time I'm going to push for my idea is if I feel that my idea is better or that their idea doesn't work for whatever reason.

Q:

You got involved immediately with *Mermaid* since you developed it. When does a director at Disney usually get involved with a project?

A:

It depends. For example *Aladdin* has been in development for a while before we ever got involved, but we're tending to start a little bit from scratch. As writers, I'd say, we would get involved fairly early. Even with *The Great Mouse Detective*, I was involved with that real early. I wasn't a director at that point, I was a storyboard artist, but I was one of the first people on that project.

Our case is unique as far as writing and directing. If we were only directing, we might get involved later after the script had been written. Possibly, there could have been a fair amount of visual development done up to that point. Although, the way things work at Disney, the projects languish a little bit until a director is involved, in the sense that a lot of work can get done,

but, in terms of actual production, that can't really happen until a director gets involved.

Q:

As a director, what do you enjoy about directing and what do you enjoy directing?

A:

I'd say the main thing I enjoy about directing is just seeing the concept become a reality. I think of myself primarily as a writer. I think I became a director because if you're just involved with the story and you're not involved with the directing, a lot of times, ideas that you had don't get realized. Certainly, the director has much more control than the writer or the storyboard artist has, and I think that's the thing I enjoy the most; having the control, making sure that an idea can get carried through to the end, and that the story that you have in mind gets up on the screen the way you think it should. There's a lot of work in directing.

I'd say, in terms of just being fun, the writing is more fun. But the directing is more satisfying because you're dealing with the actual movie. And certainly, it's thrilling to see it come to life and to see it start gaining momentum. These things take an enormous effort to get going. But once they do, they take on a life of their own somewhat. That gets (to be) fun. *Mermaid* was a tremendously difficult project to pull off. It was very stressful. It involved working long days and a lot of weekends; and enormous pressure just in terms of meeting the release date. I'd say all those things made it less than fun. It was fun when the movie was done and it did well and you felt relieved, and you felt like all the effort that had been put into it was worthwhile. Somehow, if I had known that it would be as successful as it was during production, the whole process would have been a lot more enjoyable.

I'd say *Great Mouse Detective*, for whatever reason, wasn't as much stress. It wasn't quite as ambitious a movie. It was a lighter thing that we could just have more fun with. But, *Mermaid* was, I'd say, very challenging and very difficult.

Q:

On a production, what would you say is your average daily routine?

A:

It really varies a lot because of the different stages. Right now, for example, my daily routine, at least in the last couple of weeks, has been just coming in and closing my door and sitting at a computer working on a word processor. Although that's just the writing stage, that's not the directing.

Now, we're starting to bring on some people, so we'll get more involved looking at boards, looking at character designs, visual stuff. We're tending to have a lot more meetings and that will continue the more the production gets going. We're involved with staffing at the moment, figuring out who's going to take on key areas; jobs like art direction and storyboard artist and things like that.

It's different in peak production. I'd say the heaviest work load comes at a point, probably about eight months before the film comes out, when almost all areas are going on at the same time. You're still doing some story repairs. Animation is still going on. You're heavily into clean up, you're heavily into effects

animation. You're starting to get involved with sound effects and post-production. Everything's happening at the same time. And at that point, it's kind of like working at a fast food restaurant. It's literally like you come in and it's a tornado or a whirlwind. And you're running around all day long and you feel like you can never catch up and that there's always more to do than you could ever have time to do. And it's sort of exhilarating in a sense, and you're going a lot on adrenalin. But, it literally is like that.

The way we worked on *Mermaid*, we'd have a sheet of paper on our door. Anyone who wanted to see us, put their name up and whenever we had a few moments free, we'd call whoever was highest up on the list, and then cross their name off. You just couldn't ever complete that list.

Then it starts to taper off again. When animation finishes, it gets a little easier. Then, when clean-up finishes, it's a little easier. And so on down into the final stages.

Q:

How much freedom are you given on a production?

A:

At Disney now, we work very closely with management, particularly with Jeffrey Katzenberg, who is the head of the Motion Picture Division. Jeffrey is what's called a "hands-on" executive, which means that he's very involved. I'd say we get our way a considerable amount, but we have to fight for everything. Nothing is a given and everything is challenged. You have to defend what you want and there's a great deal of input. And a lot of that input is positive. Jef-

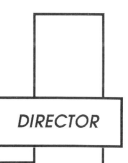

DIRECTOR

frey is a pusher. He sort of reacts instantaneously to things. Things he doesn't like, he comes down on them pretty hard. He always wants things to be better.

Of course, we have limitations with budget, and the big thing at Disney is always "faster, better, cheaper." We want all three of those things, but somehow, they're not supposed to fight against each other. So I'd say Jeffrey certainly has a lot of input and there's a lot of give and take there. He's certainly brought something to the movie. And overall, the movie is quite a bit better than if he wasn't involved. At the same time, I think that there are things that he wanted to do that, in the end, if we talked him out of it, he was glad we talked him out of it. And he's also good in the sense that if he feels that he's wrong about something, he'll back down. But if he feels like he's right, he's never going to back down. He's going to keep pushing on it. So, it's not like total artistic freedom. It's certainly not like we can do anything we want.

Certainly, the types of films that we make, they're mainly designed as entertainments. We want them to be audience pleasers and we want them to be profitable. So, they don't tend to get very self-indulgent, like, "No one's going to understand this, but I get satisfaction out of it." It's more like, we definitely want films to communicate strongly to the audience and everybody's constantly evaluating the movie. "Is it working? Is every aspect working? If it's not, why isn't it working? And what's going to make it better?"

And then, later when we go into previews where we show the film in various stages to audi-

ences, we're evaluating the audience reaction. What's going over? What's not going over? How can we make it better? But, I think we always felt, in spite of all that, with *Mermaid*, we were making the film we wanted to make. We didn't feel we were being forced into doing something we didn't want to do.

Q:
On the personal side, what project or production has given you the most professional satisfaction and enjoyment, and why?
A:

I would say, *The Little Mermaid* has been the most satisfying project that I've been involved with. For some of the reasons I mentioned before, it was such a difficult film and there were certainly points during the course of production where we thought that, a) it's not going to work, or b) we're not going to get it done in time. I mean, there are things that I'm not happy with and there are things that I feel could've been a lot better, but generally, I think, under the circumstances, that it worked well. And we were pleased to get it done in time. No one really cares about that except us, but there were some miraculous aspects to that, and it had to do with people going above and beyond the call of duty and doing work beyond what we felt we could really ask of them. And so there's something very satisfying about that.

Beyond that, it's just nice to have a movie come out that people have heard of and they've seen and they've enjoyed. I mean, I've been at Disney for 16-and-a-half years and some of the things I've worked on, I like better than others. But a lot of times, you go, "Is anybody that I know going to see these things?" *Great Mouse Detective*, I liked a lot, too, and I was genuinely disappointed that it wasn't seen by more people. And there are various reasons for that, that go beyond the film. Some involved the way the film was marketed and the time it was released. But, it certainly is a lot nicer to have your work widely exposed. And you feel much more like it was worth the effort, because it is a tremendous effort that goes into these things.

Q:

Conversely, what was a project you worked on that may have been successful commercially or critically, but that you felt didn't live up to what you wanted?

A:

Of all the projects I've been involved with, I think I was most disappointed with *The Black Cauldron*. Although I wasn't involved with that all through production, I was involved fairly early in the story. I was certainly very excited about *The Black Cauldron* and thought it had potential to be a tremendous movie. In some sense I felt that it could go beyond anything that had ever been done and I was disappointed with the way it turned out. Although there are a lot of beautiful things in the movie. I don't think story was its strongest suit.

Q:

Being a director, can you name an animated film or two that you think was well directed and one that you think the directing seemed to lag on?

A:

I'll talk about Disney films in

both cases. *Pinocchio* is, I think, a brilliant movie. And that was the movie that had the biggest impact on me when I was a kid. I mean, it goes beyond direction. It goes into every area, but I think direction is a part of that. I think, in terms of the staging and the animation, that it's a triumphant movie and a monumental effort. Sort of a sense of people just going beyond. I think *Snow White* is great and then, *Pinocchio* was going one step further and everybody reaching for the limits. I think that's one of my favorite movies.

The Disney film that had just been released before I started working at Disney, was *Robin Hood*. I'd say that film is not one of the most successful in terms of cohesiveness. I think it has a sort of episodic aspect to it and a feeling of sequences being moved from the beginning to the end and the middle. And, as a result, it doesn't pull together as well as some of the best ones do.

Q:

If you were starting in the business today, how would you prepare yourself for doing what you're doing?

A:

It's interesting. I'd say, directing, itself, is becoming, at least at Disney, more of an attractive prospect for people and there are more people that want to get into directing. And that's a little different than it used to be. Disney's always been more or less focused on the animators, unlike Warner Brothers, where everybody knows the directors, like Chuck Jones and Friz Freleng and Bob Clampett. And people don't tend to know the animators as well, even though there's brilliant animation in those shorts.

DIRECTOR

With Disney, it's always been the animators. The directing animator or supervising animator has always been considered almost more the key position, or at least, the well known position. And you know all the great Disney animators, like Frank Thomas, Ollie Johnston, Milt Kahl, Freddy Moore, and Bill Tytla, and none of the directors, even though they did really good work, like Dave Hand or... (pause) See? I rest my case. They tend to be more anonymous. I guess that was because Walt was more the dominant figure. Nowadays, we're getting a sense that animation directing is becoming more prestigious like in live action.

However, if your sight is in directing, per se, you're not likely to be able to move right into that. You're more likely to get into that from some related area. As I say, my background and John's background is similar. It's animation and story. And I think that's actually a pretty good sort of background for an animation director because in some sense, you're trying to use the animation to tell the story.

As far as getting into those areas, certainly, now is a good time. Who knows what's going to happen in the next few years, but right now is a booming time for animation with TV's *The Simpsons* and *Mermaid* and everything. There are a lot more features in the works. Disney certainly is expanding all the time.

And I think that the basics haven't changed that much. Drawing ability is important. Creative ability is important. A sense of entertainment. I think Cal Arts is probably still the best overall training, in terms of a school. As far as their character

animation program, I think it is the most comprehensive. And the people that come out of there have the best training. A majority of the people at Disney come out of the Cal Arts program.

Beyond that, it's important just to set your sights clearly. There's certainly a lot of areas to get into in animation, if that's what someone wants. But, I think you need to focus and set a clear goal, a specific goal, and then, work really hard to get it. If you sort of want to do this, or maybe that or something over here, then I think it's a lot harder to be successful.

From THE LITTLE MERMAID—
Top: Ariel and Ursula, the sea witch
Bottom: King Triton and Sebastian

© *Walt Disney Co.*

Darrell Van Citters

DATE: JULY 18, 1990

Q:
Please give a brief description of your career including studios and projects you've worked on.
A:
I was an art school major for the first year of college. After that I came out to California Institute of the Arts for three years. I worked one summer at Chuck Jones' studio as inbetweener/gofer. The next summer I spent as an assistant at Filmation Studios. I graduated with a B.F.A. and went straight into the animation business. The summer after that I started at Walt Disney Studio as a trainee in animation. I worked up from trainee to assistant animator, or animating assistant, and up to animator and we'll just say I ended up doing story

on some TV specials, which led me to directing and I've been directing since about 1981.

I was an animator on *The Fox and the Hound* and did story and direction on *Fun with Mr. Future*. It was not exclusive story credit, though. Then came development on the ill-fated *Who Framed Roger Rabbit*. Last at Disney was direction on the *Sport Goofy* film called *Soccermania*. I was freelance for three years between Disney and Warner Brothers, working on a multitude of commercials. Now I'm with Warner Brothers as the creative director of their animation department.

Q:
So you broke in as Chuck Jones' gofer and inbetweener?

A:

No, I really broke in in 1974 as a cel painter at this little tiny commercial studio in Albuquerque, NM. I worked as a cel painter, Xerox technician, finally doing some assistant work for one of their house freelance animators. I tried to find out about Cal Arts and went from there. So I started right at the bottom.

Q:

What does a directing animator do?

A:

Directing animator or animation director?

Q:

Both. And the difference.

A:

A directing animator is basically a position, for example at the Disney Studio, where you're the head animator for a group of animators, on a sequence or a character or something like that. The director over at a place like Disney would supervise all the directing animators for the entire production. A director over here at Warner Brothers is a lot closer to dealing with the individual artists in that the director here will do character layouts, exposure sheet timings and oversee the animation as it's done. I work directly with the animators to get the scenes on the screen the way they were envisioned.

Q:

Would you say it is similar to what is called the "classic shorts period" in animation at Warners?

161

A:

In terms of the job I do, yes. My directing is very similar to that. At Disney my understanding is that the directors don't have the time to do the actual character layouts and exposure sheets. They work directly with the animator when they hand out a scene, but they don't give the same kind of information up front. The animator will come back with that information after the fact and see if his vision jibes with the director's.

Q:

How much supervision do you feel is necessary?

A:

It depends on the staff. I try to hire the best people I can so that I don't have to be supervising them that much. Once I give them the layouts and the exposure sheet and we've talked it over, they're on their own. My job basically is not to animate for them; my job is to just guide them, make sure that the overall whole works.

Q:

When do you generally get involved with a project?

A:

At the very beginning, working on the story with the writer or the storyman. That's because if the director doesn't see it, it isn't going to make it on the screen. And as a director, as well as with a producer, you see it from the very beginning to the very end. And I think when you're involved with something that long, you really want to feel like you believe in it.

Q:

You work with basically all

the areas: writer, voices?

A:

All the way up through post-production.

Q:

Do you cast the voices?

A:

It's a tricky, tricky thing over at Warner Brothers. I have input on who gets cast in the voices, but I don't actually cast the voices.

Q:

In other productions you've worked on?

A:

Yes. It would be a combination of the director and producer casting the voices.

Q:

What are your strongest areas in direction? Where do you feel you are a good director?

A:

Hmm, I'd say in comedy timing and in guiding the animators so that they do things clearly and simply. Not simplistically, but simply so that they achieve clarity. And hopefully inspiring them.

Q:

You mention comedy timing. What is your definition of that? Maybe an example would help.

A:

I think comedy timing is knowing how quickly or how slowly to do something to optimize its comedic impact. Sometimes very slow timing can be considered comedy timing, and at the same time very quick timing can be considered comedy timing. That's what most people usually associate with it, but sometimes you can get a bigger laugh by a very drawn-out reaction to something. Or even no animation is a reaction to something. Does that make any sense?

Q:

Yes, it does. What is your average routine on a production?

A:

The daily routine changes the farther along you get in the picture, obviously. You're no longer doing layouts. The guys are all animating and your daily routine is different. You spend most of your time looking at tests on the video to see if the animation is working.

Q:

Let's start at the beginning of production and sort of go step-by-step.

A:

At the very beginning I will take the storyboards and figure out if the way we've got it staged in the storyboard is the best way to stage it. And if it can be improved upon, I'll sketch in really crude layouts in terms of perspective or angles or things like that. Next comes the character layouts on top of those. And then my background layouts, the perspective planes and things like that, will go to the background layout person or production designer and he'll work over those things to give it "the look."

Q:

What is the difference between character layout and background layout?

A:

Background layout is just the setting. The character layout is the characters themselves fitting in that setting. Once I've decided what the angle is, what the setting is going to be—I don't worry so much about designing that, I just know where the characters will be placed within that, and I let the background layout person take care of that. With character stuff you deal with as many poses as you need in the scene to get the idea across. When you have a steady crew of animators, you can develop a shorthand where you don't have to use quite as many poses.

Q:

Would that be like key animation?

A:

Yes. You just give them the poses that tell the story. Sometimes you'll need to add a little bit more than was present in the storyboard itself. I prefer not to give them too many poses. I don't want to animate the scene for them. I'd like them to bring something to it that I can't put into it. That's part of their job. And it's expressions, it's little movements, things like that that you add just to fill out the storyboard, basically.

From there, once we have the dialogue recorded, I will take those poses and roughly expose them on an exposure sheet and show the animators where I want the timings to occur. They have a lot of flexibility in the timings and we work out the fine points once they've started animating the scene and we see it on the video. Then we can see what's working clearly, what could use more improvement in the timing, or where we could use a little more elegance in the timing.

So once I've done the character layouts, I've got the stuff on the exposure sheets, given them timings, I'll issue the scenes and we'll discuss what kind of acting we're trying for in

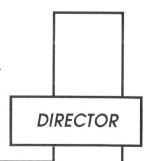

DIRECTOR

this scene. What kind of timing we're trying for. Whether we want to push the comedy end of it or whether we don't want to push at all. We will discuss the whole scene inside and out. Then he or she will go away with the scene and do it in a very rough form and show it to me on the animation video camera.

I look to see if the person's going the right direction, if they ought to continue to keep breaking it down and making the animation more fluid and timed the way we discussed it. This continues until both of us agree on the way the scene has come out. I'll tell the animator to go ahead and draw it out so it can be followed up by an assistant animator, and the process repeats itself from there.

Q:

At which point it eventually goes to a pencil test.

A:

Yes. Once we see it, roughly drawn on the video, it will go to the assistant animators and they will do the cleaned-up drawings, and then we send that out to the camera services room and get that shot on film so that we can not only double-check the animation on it, but double-check the way it was drawn, too. This is to make sure there's nothing out of the ordinary or out of arc. We're trying to eliminate glitches every step of the way. That's just another part of the fail-safe, another redundancy in the system, or whatever you want to call it. It's just a quality control step. Once you see it on film, the actual drawings, you can tell if there's going to be any problems with it projected on a large screen. That's the last chance you have to make any corrections before it

goes to color. Then the corrections get expensive.

Q:

How involved are you in the color process?

A:

I'll discuss that with the production designer or background people, but I try not to get too involved with that. I try to hire people who know what they're doing in that department and let them do what they feel is appropriate. I'll just come in after they've done their work and I'll either make suggestions or okay it. Basically I don't like to tell anyone what to do on a picture. I figure I'm hiring them to do a job, and I want them to do the job they're hired to do. All I do is edit or guide.

Q:

Do you go into the actual editing process at the end?

A:

It's animation editing, so it's basically gluing scenes together. There really isn't much creativity in the editing process. You can fine-tune some of your cuts and animation—I won't say animation, you'll fine-tune some of your actual editing by shortening scenes or things like that in the process, but basically animation picture editing is just gluing scenes together. Then I'll work with the sound effects editor, work with the mixers who mix the final soundtrack and get the levels right. But most basically, animation editing is done as you draw it.

Q:

You've directed numerous films from shorts to commercials. How much freedom are you given on an average production, like a commercial?

A:

Damn little. On a commercial a client is selling product and you're there to help sell product. So you do what he wants done on a commercial. When you're working on a theatrical production, you are still selling a product, that is the character which helps sell licensed merchandise. But you have a little more leeway. You're able to tell a story and you don't have that limitation of 30 seconds to tell the beginning, middle and end of the story.

You're given a fair amount of freedom, at least here at Warner Brothers. Of course everybody all the way up and down the ladder has input into it. We have been fortunate, here, that everybody tends to agree on the type of film we're making. Warner's is a little trickier because you have such a vast library of major history here that you're working with, which is both liberating and confining at the same time.

It's liberating in that you have these characters with a lot of dimension to them; it's a wonderful precedent. Confining in that you want to bring your stamp to it too, you don't want to duplicate what the master directors have done in the past. Disney studios, I think, has probably a little less freedom on a picture, but I think you'll find that out when you talk to the Disney animators, what their feelings are like there. I generally had a fair amount of freedom there, but then I was working on projects that management really didn't care that much about, so I was not doing any high-profile projects. Features are where you have a little less freedom, I think.

Q:

What project, work, film or commercial have you worked on that you really were totally satisfied with?

A:

I probably never am totally satisfied with anything I've ever worked on. I think the short *Fun with Mr. Future* was a lot of fun to make because it was kind of busting loose after working on a project that was as staid as *Fox and Hound*. We kind of got a chance to play. We got to discover for ourselves comedy timing and there really weren't any rules in that picture. It was a lot of fun to do. We were just kind of let loose and we had a good time making it.

Q:

On the opposite spectrum, what is a project you've been involved with that you felt failed? It may not have been a commercial failure or critical failure, but you personally felt that it didn't meet the expectations?

A:

I have to be careful in that. I'd say a failed project was the *Sport Goofy* film. In that one you were taking a klutz, a world-renowned klutz, Goofy, and suddenly making him very good at sports. Which, as a concept, is pretty thin. And beyond that, it was started with one regime and finished under another. And we all know what happens when that occurs.

Q:

Most of the "golden age" animators began working on short subjects and eventually graduated to feature work. You have done the reverse. You basically made your start in feature films and now you're working on

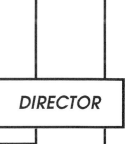

DIRECTOR

theatrical shorts. *Do you have any comment over this evolution, or de-evolution?*

A:

I can't say it's really a de-evolution. I think there's some people who feel more comfortable in one medium, whether it's features or shorts, than another. I personally wouldn't want to break it up into doing shorts or features. For me, it's been an evolution in that I find shorts or short projects rewarding, because you can always try something different since every few months your desk is being cleaned off, and you can start on something fresh.

On a feature, once you commit to something, you're two or three years in the process. And even if you've got a better idea, you've got to wait until that film is done. And as a film evolves, you find out, "Well, gee, now we should go back and re-do that because I've got a better way of doing it." But you can't. You have to wait and finish the film. Whereas with a short, or the short project, your turnover is that much faster and you can take what you learned out of that one and apply it to the next one very quickly.

Q:

Since you have moved up the ladder from actually cel painter to director and producer, is there a particular aspect of animation that you enjoy the most? Some task you would do for no money?

A:

Well this is a business. (laughs) There's probably nothing I would do for no money. I enjoy what I'm doing right now. I like animating, but I enjoy doing poses for the animators and working with the animators and

that in itself is fun. But I also like handing it to the animators and having them come back and surprise me with something that—I have to be careful how I say this—I don't like being shocked. I like when an animator *adds* something unexpected to a scene. He adds a little bit of life to it that you hadn't planned on. When I do character layouts, I'm not trying to restrict an animator's work. But there's a time and money factor when you're doing the short projects. Things have to be delineated as clearly as possible so they can go through as quickly and smoothly as possible. But within that, the animator can still manage to add a little touch, sometimes a big touch, that really makes a scene shine. I really like working with people and having them bring back something more than what I handed out. That's a real thrill, because you really feel like something's building there. I don't want people to do exactly what I say. I'm giving them guidelines and the thrill for me is seeing them come back with more. And it works real well that way. We build it as a team.

Q:

How do you judge animation direction in general? What do you think is a well-directed animated film, short, or whatever?

A:

(Laughs) You're going to get me into trouble, aren't you?

I think, first of all in general terms, a lot of animated commercials are not successful in animation or filmmaking terms because you usually have to put 10 pounds of "stuff" in a five-pound bag. You've got so much information to convey in such a short amount of time and the clients want the world on the head of a pin, so you get poor staging or over-active staging. You have too many cuts in a 30-second period.

Clients tend to think that full animation is good animation. So everything is done fully, but that doesn't necessarily mean clearly. I like very cartoony animation, but by the same token, I won't use it gratuitously and I won't use it for its own sake. I like restraint in my animation. Control. So that when the funny stuff, the wild stuff happens, it pays off.

Sometimes the funniest animation is no animation. I think one scene that stood out for me above all the scenes in, for example, *Great Mouse Detective* [Disney, 1986], was the scene with Ratigan when he's talking to Basil, and looking at his pocket watch. Basil replies to him. You can see that whatever Basil said to Ratigan didn't go over well. There was that pause. Just a held drawing, but you can see the wheels spin in the Ratigan's head. Then he just closes the cover of the watch. To me that was good timing and there was absolutely no motion in there, but you could see the wheels spinning in this character's head. To me that's what it's about. It's not how many drawings you use, it's which ones you use and how you use them.

I think there are some real nice moments in *Little Mermaid*. There's a lot of clarity and good use of animation timing and camera in that film. There's not a lot of shorts going on right now so I can't really comment on that. I think when you see *Box Office Bunny* you'll see that there's some wilder stuff and there's quieter stuff. I try to restrain it so that you've got someplace to go when you want to do the more outrageous things.

Q:
What film do you think has bad direction?
A:
I think it might be better to keep it general. I do have to work in this town.

Q:
If you were starting today in the business or giving advice to someone who was interested in getting into animation, what would you tell them?
A:
Well, we had Mike Maltese [key writer for Warner Brothers and Hanna-Barbera] up to Cal Arts to lecture. Somebody brought that kind of thing up to him. He said, "If my kid wanted to get into the business, first thing I'd do is break his pencil, then break his arm."

I don't know, I wouldn't know what to tell somebody how to prepare to get into this business. You better love drawing. You really better love it. To the point where even when it gets tedious, you still love it. Animation is a lot of hard work. It's not one of those professions for the misty-eyed. It's a lot of work, and even if you've got a vision, you've got to remember you're working in a commercial operation and a lot of your vision will be subordinated to support that commercial operation. But if you can handle all that, it's worth doing.

It's kind of amazing to be able to do all these funny drawings and have somebody pay you lots of money for it. And it's a lot of fun to create the illusion of life where there was none, to bring characters to life, that are really just a bunch of drawings.

DIRECTOR

Go to art school, enjoy drawing, enjoy cartooning. If you're going to be in animation, I think it would be nice if you had a real understanding for drawing cartoons. And observe everything around you, constantly. Constantly. Be interested in everything around you. It all comes in handy, because animation is really just observation, both technically and artistically. It's observing the actions and attitudes and personalities around you, and commenting on those. So the observation is an extremely important part of it.

Opposite: Model drawings from MAD SCIENTIST, a proposed EPCOT film which later became FUN WITH MR. FUTURE © *Walt Disney Productions*

This Page: From BOX OFFICE FUNNY © *Warner Bros.*

DIRECTOR

Gary Goldman

Gary Goldman is one of the trio that forms the creative side of Sullivan Bluth in Ireland. Originally one of Disney's new hopes of the Seventies, he left the studio with Don Bluth to create one of the most discussed studios of the Eighties. Though now officially a producer, Goldman continues drawing almost on a daily basis in an attempt to maintain what he, Don Bluth and John Pomeroy have christened Classical Animation. Gary had been Atlantic hopping, handling work in Ireland and voice direction in Los Angeles. We finally caught up with him via phone directly at his office in Ireland.

DATE: AUGUST 23, 1990

Q:
Can you give a brief description of your career in the business, including studios you've worked at and productions you've worked on?
A:
After I graduated from art school in Hawaii and returned to the mainland, California, I went to see Lee Holly, the artist who does a cartoon strip called "Ponytail," that's nationally syndicated. He liked my portfolio, but he thought what might help me in the area of cartooning would be to go to Los Angeles and get involved in animation. I didn't want to go to Los Angeles, but I did. I, as most young artists would, took my portfolio around to the different animation studios.

At DePatie-Freleng, the receptionist wouldn't let me in. She said everybody was on lay-off. I said, "Why don't you ask the producer if he'd look at my portfolio?" Ed Love was there and he looked at my portfolio and directed me to Disney. So I began, at Disney, as a trainee in February of 1972. I spent the next seven-and-a-half years of my animation career there. That is where I met Don [Bluth] and John Pomeroy.

I worked as an inbetweener and eventually as assistant to Frank Thomas on *Robin Hood*. I worked as an animator on *Winnie the Pooh and Tigger Too* and on *The Rescuers* under the direction of the late John Lounsbery. I was directing animator on *Pete's Dragon* and *The Small One* un-

der Don Bluth's direction. Just before we left Disney, we were working on *The Fox and the Hound* as directing animators. We took no credit on that film.

In 1979, we resigned our positions at Disney to start our own company, where I've worked as producer and directing animator, scene planner, cameraman, editor (wearing several hats) on *Banjo the Woodpile Cat*. We finished it in 1979 and it was released in two theaters (The Egyptian Theater, in Hollywood, and The Pine Tree Theater, in Northridge) for Academy Award consideration. It was licensed to NBC for two showings, but it was not aired until the summer of 1982.

I worked as a producer, directing animator, and scene planner on *The Secret of Nimh*. I didn't animate, but I coordinated the work on *Xanadu* as a scene planner and line producer for the *Xanadu* animation. On *Dragon's Lair*, *Space Age* and *Dragon's Lair II*, I actually worked as a producer. I did not animate on any one of those three projects.

In late 1984 we started *An American Tail*. On that picture I worked as the co-direction producer and sort of a co-director, but we did not take credit. The same roles were assumed on *The Land Before Time* (1988). I was producer and co-director on *All Dogs Go to Heaven* (1989) and *Rock-A-Doodle* (1990). We're currently completing *Rock-A-Doodle* and are also heavily into animation on *A Troll in Central Park*.

Scene from THE SECRET OF NIMH animated by Gary Goldman

Q:

What art training did you have, if any?

A:

I went to Cabrillo Junior College in Northern California. My major was drawing and art. I went on to the University of Hawaii, where I majored in life drawing and minored in art history. My major in life drawing was suggested by Warner Brothers' Animation Director Robert McKimson. I had gone to visit him after receiving an Associate of Arts Degree and showed him a portfolio. Warner Brothers Animation was on a lay-off period. He had advised me to continue my art training and come back with the same kind of portfolio, but with more life drawing experience.

He said, "Please do *not* bring me any cartoon drawings, don't bring me any designs, if you bring me back a strong drawing portfolio, I'll hire you and I'll train you how to do what we do." In 1969, it was difficult to find a school that would actually offer life drawing as a major, but I was accepted at six schools, including The Rhode Island School of Design, Oakland Arts and Crafts and the University of Washington.

I had also applied to Chouinard. It was before Cal Arts was formed. They were transferring the school from Chouinard, in downtown Los Angeles, out to Cal Arts, in Valencia, and were not taking any new applicants.

The University of Hawaii was recommended to me by an artist whom I'd known since I was a child. She was a family friend and a very well-known oil painter living in the San Jose/San Francisco area. She felt that the school offered some really great training including professional painters, artists and sculptors who are making it in today's commercial world. Some made guest appearances at the school; Chagall, Wayne Thiebaud, just to name a couple. Chagall would set up printmaking. He would do printmaking for six weeks and the students could actually observe the way he approached it and ask questions while he was working. They did the same with Wayne Thiebaud in the painting department.

I went on a crash course to get through the last two years of art school in 16 months. I came out with a fairly strong portfolio, the one I took to Ed Love. Out of six different studios, he was the only one that looked at my portfolio until I submitted it to Disney. I waited for three anxious days until they called and said I had won myself a position in their training program.

It was there, during that first week, that I met Don and formed a friendship and love for animation. It was a year later, almost to the day, that I met John as he walked through the door at Disney. I think both Don and I recognized that John had the same kind of fever for preserving that classical element which attracted us to Disney in the first place.

Q:

What does a producer do in the big picture of animation?

A:

I don't really know. All I can talk about is our case. I would say, if you referred to the way that Don, John and I take that title, it's more like a line producer, in that we're totally active in the motion picture production. I still draw daily; not scenes that I've been assigned, but over the top of scenes that animators and directing animators are working on.

Our roles go from choosing the composer who will write the score for the picture, the song writers, approaching script writers, scripting a story that may have originated here, being involved with the story and selection of stories we're going to produce, approaching the actors and their agents and attending the voice sessions where we're directing the voices. We're sort of producers-cum-directors. We also maintain a teaching role. We're passing on many of the things we've learned how to do to younger artists and administrators within the company who will become producers or production supervisors, directing animators, department heads, etc.

I'd say our involvement is actually all the way through production. I'm still doing things like sweatboxing scenes as a director and approving scenes that are going to go to Xerox and approving final color; right on down to supervising the final dub with the supervising sound editor and color-correcting the picture.

Q:

When you search for new property, what do you look for in that as a producer?

A:

I think that all three of us might end up saying the same thing. I think that number one is a strong story. We may have hit or missed in our past, but to us we're looking for a strong story with strong entertaining value. We're also looking for something with an interesting or different twist so it doesn't have someone pointing a finger at it saying, "It's just like *Snow White*," or

one of the other classics created by Walt Disney which have been the hallmarks up to now.

Q:

Once you've decided on a property, what are the first steps to starting up a production?

A:

We're currently a trained organization with 460 people. But, if we were starting from scratch, as we did on *The Secret of Nimh*, it was basically our very small crew of about 19 people, 19 key people whose skill levels we knew. You might even refer to it as kind of a nepotism because once you know them and you become friends with them, you find yourself counting on their skills and loyalty to help you do the production.

On *Nimh,* we actually started an all-out recruiting campaign. It wasn't anything we had to really work hard at because the publicity about our departure from Disney excited an awful lot of people in the animation industry and just about everybody came running to us. We have 21 departments, from storyboard all the way through color production camera. You need a certain amount of people in each of those departments to achieve your weekly quotas so as to meet your deadline and budget. So, the first thing, when you start a production, is to figure out what story you're going to do and how long you think it's going to be (the number of minutes). Then you get down to some mechanics about how much can 'x' number of animators produce, per week, to get the picture animated. Then you've got to find a specific number of animators that can do 'x' amount of footage per week.

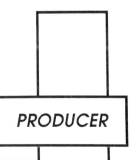

PRODUCER

Nowadays, animators average somewhere between seven and 10 feet a week. At the time we did *Secret of Nimh*, those who eventually became key directing animators, Linda Miller, Lorna Pomeroy and Dan Kuenster, were all animating somewhere between three and four feet per week. John [Pomeroy] was capable of animating consistently 12 to 15 feet per week. If he was really burning the midnight oil, he could do as much as 30 feet a week. *Nimh* was animated by only 11 of us.

Don storyboarded the entire picture and he animated the two-minute fight sequence between Justin and Jenner. In fact, Don storyboarded, with the exception of two or three sequences in *The Land Before Time*, all of our pictures. It wasn't until *All Dogs Go to Heaven* that he released a lot of the boarding to other people. Now we've got about a 12-member storyboard team.

Basically you need to fill pre-production and leadership roles. When you're wearing the producer's hat you're looking at the first part of the production for ways of how you're going to get the production finished. You need to fill the leadership roles, in each department, with people who will inspire the crew, people whom you, as a producer, can depend on. Our struggle is to keep the crew happy and satisfied on a day-to-day basis. It's pretty much a hard-nosed drive all the way through. I've always looked at the director and the producer's jobs as servants to the crew. Even though the producer and director positions, at least to the crew, appear to be the Lord high Poobah [from Gilbert and Sullivan's *Mikado*,] when you're in those shoes, you'll find the job

can get quite uncomfortable. But with the right leaders, production can run smoothly. It's finding the right people, with some or a lot of experience, that is difficult. We've found that training our own crew is best. We have a great Irish crew as well as an experienced American and Canadian animation staff.

Q:
When you're gathering your staff, what sort of people do you look for?
A:
In our case I think we look for people who are artistically productive. We look for people who have flair. We're looking for people with strong drawing ability because an animator, a layout man, a storyboard artist or a background artist, are limited by their creative craft or skill level. They're limited by how well they can actually draw or paint. We're looking for both those who are experienced and for potential animation talent. Also people who want to do animation, it takes a lot of drive to conquer this medium and a lot of stamina.

Q:
On an average day, what do you do at the studio?
A:
On an average day I come to the studio at between 6 and 7 in the morning and I leave between 7:30 and 9 at night. That's just *my* hours. We take a short break for lunch. I think all three of us are in the same boat.

My day starts off usually on a steenback or a movieola and I try to spend those early morning hours, before the crew arrives at 9, doing, what I call, "sweat-boxing." This is more wearing the director's hat. I will approve scenes to go into Clean-Up, or review scenes to be approved to go to Xerox (the final process after you've had clean-up and effects animated and shot on black and white film as a pencil test). I approve color scenes to be cut in and readied for negative assembly.

At 9 o'clock the crew arrives. I am then heavily involved with the animators all day long. The animators need attention or approval on a video or to flip their scene. I give them approval to have their scenes completed by their assistants and inbetweeners. I may spend most of my morning and afternoon in a directional mode. There are story meetings and meetings where we're deciding on who's going to do what as voices, or song writers, etc. There is scheduling, working with the production manager and accountants on where we stand on the motion picture, what can we do to cut the costs, how can we inspire the crew, how can we meet our weekly deadline or it might be that we have eight weeks left to deliver the project. We're usually in meetings or on the phone together about how we might solve the problem in the production.

I've never seen any production without a daily problem in its schedule or meeting its budgetary requirements. In many cases, you end up making decisions where you have to cut either story content, production value or eliminate a song you've already paid for. You have to wear two hats in this area, too. You have a "creative integrity" hat you have on and you also have a "marketing" hat that you must wear with your investor and the distributor of the film. You might want to hold your integrity to something you feel is quite beautiful on the screen, but you might have to alter it to achieve commercial success.

Those are the hardest decisions to make because you have to answer to yourself, morally. You also have to answer those artists who have fallen in love with certain things in the motion picture. Since most of the artists are adults and we're creating a medium for the genre that spans from three-and-a-half-year-old to the grannies and grandpas out there, we have to acknowledge the fact that many of the audience are very, very young. Sometimes we show our dark side. Some of the most artful things to us are on the dark side.

I'd say my daily routine spans being a producer where I'm talking to an agent, a scriptwriter, a songwriter or an actor. Securing an artist's interest in working with us on a film, actually drawing on an animated scene or going down to camera to see how a particular scene is coming along. Your interest in those scenes and those crew members who are doing those jobs is instrumental to creating inspiration to those facing daily quotas. It's important that people know you care, not just about the film but about what they are doing.

Q:
How much freedom are you usually given on a production?
A:
We've been probably more fortunate than most people in an independent film production nature. The most limited I think we've ever been on freedom would probably be on *Land Before Time*. But, on *American Tail* we actually had total freedom.

PRODUCER

All Steven asked for was approval of the storyboards and the script. He only requested a couple of changes. In most cases it was either accepted or he'd come back with an idea that might be a little bit better or different that he liked better. On *Secret of Nimh*, we basically had total creative control and freedom. As a producer or director, people think you have freedom because you can do it any way you want. But when you're actually standing in those shoes, you're limited by the 24-hour day. That's the biggest limitation on your freedom.

Money is freedom. However there's a moral aspect of how much money you're going to spend on a motion picture.

Q:

How much freedom do you usually give on an average production?

A:

I would say that we've been pretty tight creatively. In the last year or two we've become quite generous with the animators. If it's a really top animator, we'll give plenty of room, but we still give plenty of direction or, at least, approvals. With the composer, we're pretty free, but most composers who have worked with us have liked the way we track the picture. The term, tracking the picture, is the selection of music from other productions to give the film a mood, or the sequence a mood to inspire the animator.

Jerry Goldsmith, on *Secret of Nimh*, would not, at first, look at the film with its tracking music. (He wanted to look at it with dialogue only.) When his music editor came, he called Jerry and said "I think you'll like what they've done, why don't you look at it with their tracking music." It's been basically the same throughout all five productions, including *Rock-A-Doodle*. We give enough information to the composer about what we want to hear in the music spotting sessions. We try to use synonyms and adjectives that give the composer an idea of what we're trying to convey to the audience in each sequence. Then we're basically stuck with whatever he brings back. There have only been two times in the five pictures, I can recall, where we've asked them to alter something. In both cases the composers made the changes in less than five minutes and altered the music cue significantly.

So, freedom-wise, for the crew it's pretty tight except for the storyboard artists and the key animators. The rest of the animators are usually anywhere from trainee to borderline journeymen. There are three to five what we refer to as "top animators," usually the directing animators, on a project. These top animators usually can tune into what you're trying to achieve and try to plus it. As the artists achieve higher skills they also receive more freedom.

Q:

What project have you worked on that's given you the most professional enjoyment or satisfaction, and why?

A:

I'd have to say *The Secret of Nimh*. I still think it's our best project, both for its artistic value and the sophisticated story that we tried to tell. But mostly for the enjoyment of that crew at that time. We were all young and we shared two-and-a-half years of absolute crusading, some hard times and some really good times that are extremely memorable to me. I can see scenes in that picture that still give me an emotional twinge. (I personally was involved with every single scene in the picture, either the scene planning, directing another animator, animating a scene myself, or actually shooting on the camera late night there in Studio City.)

During the last six months of that picture we were averaging somewhere near a 110 hours a week, from 6 in the morning until 11 at night. It took a big chunk out of our lives but the experience gave me so much as a learning experience and a people experience that I find it was the most satisfying. On the other projects political negatives came along that made them not as enjoyable as *The Secret of Nimh* was. Not that *Secret of Nimh* wasn't without its problems, but it was a heck of a learning experience.

Q:

If you were trying to break into the business today, how would you prepare yourself for that?

A:

I have children between the ages of 16 and 25 and I'm watching them grow and watching them all at different levels. (They're in high school and college and the oldest one is actually one of the editors here at Sullivan Bluth.) You're so limited at that age with how much you have to offer, I would think I would concentrate on my education and on improving my drawing ability. If I wanted to be an animator, I would put everything I knew how to do and all of my hours into practicing drawing so that I conquered the skill. I think that your most prolific animators are your best draftsmen. The Linda Millers, the John Pomeroys, Don Bluth, himself. Lorna Pomeroy-Cook has a complete command of that pencil and she can make it do what she wants to do. Dan Kuenster is very talented.

They're all going to be stars because they can make that pencil work for them. If I were to advise a young person who was 15 or 16 and looking at animation, I would push them to go to an art school. I'm not just talking about a well rounded education, but one that also made them draw. There are so many experiences in life that will help make a good animator. It's those experiences, the ups and down and jerks along the way, that give you emotion to put in those scenes and bring those characters to life. But,

Animation drawing from THE SECRET OF NIMH by Goldman

© *Mrs. Brisby Ltd.*

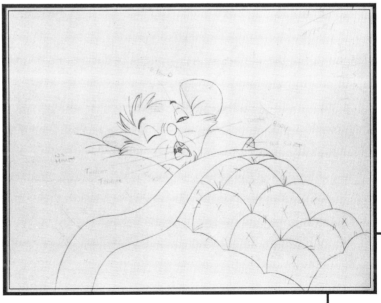

you're not going to bring them to life if you can't draw.

PRODUCER

Scott Shaw!

DATE: JULY 17, 1990

Q:
Could you please give a brief description of your career and your background, listing specific projects?

A:

I started out when I was in college, doing underground comic books, writing and drawing. And of course I had been doing strips for the school newspaper and stuff in junior high and high school. And from underground comics, I was hired by Hanna-Barbera to work on their comic book line that Marvel Comics was publishing. I started out as an inker and then did some penciling, and even writing. Studio supervisors took notice of my work and asked me if I wanted to come in and work on the Flintstones show, which they had re-vived. This was in 1978, I believe. I said "sure." The Flintstones were the characters that got me interested in being a cartoonist in the first place. I was a nine-year-old kid in 1960 and the perfect age to become fascinated with their original series.

There was discussion whether to hire me as a character designer or a layout artist. I took layout and wound up working with people that went back in the business all the way to having worked on *Snow White* and *Pinocchio* and things like that. It was really one of the last times where you could work with people that really had a lot of experience under their belt.

I was in layout there for four years, and worked on the Flintstones. Actually, it was called *The New Fred and Barney Show*.

playhouse pictures

DINO (ON ROLLERBLADES) ROLLS TOWARD CAMERA PAST ADMIRING KIDS... (THEIR HEADS TRACK DINO'S MOVEMENTS)

HE LEANS BACK AND SKATES ON HIS TAIL... IN F.G., BARNEY SPEAKS AND WINKS TO CAMERA, CONFIDENTIAL

PAN PAST BARNEY (IN F.G.) AND O.S. WITH DINO

FRED (V.O.): NEW DINO PEBBLES CEREAL! BARNEY: WITH MARSHMALLOWS!

Then I worked on *Scooby-Doo*, *Smurfs*, *Popeye*, *Casper* and a lot of typical Saturday morning productions at the time. Animation was still being done in-house on most of those series, so I would actually get to work with the animators and with other layout men and that prepared me for a lot of things to come.

Then I got back into doing comic books. I left animation for about two years and worked for DC Comics on *Captain Carrot and His Amazing Zoo Crew*. The low page rates drove me back into animation, where I worked for the mythical Tom Carter Pro-

ductions and then went to Marvel Productions as a storyboard supervisor and model supervisor on *Jim Henson's Muppet Babies*. After four years there, I went back to Hanna-Barbera, initially as a character designer, then a writer, and then was assigned my first producing job, which was on a show called *The Completely Mental Misadventures of Ed Grimley*. It was an animated version of Martin Short's character from *SCTV* and *Saturday Night Live*.

I'd also started doing a lot of commercials, and in that I had done storyboarding, layouts and

Storyboard from a Pebbles Cereal commercial drawn by Shaw!

Characters © *Hanna-Barbera Productions*

character design and some direction, not to mention dealing with non-cartoonist clients, and that prepared me for producing as well. I went over to DIC, where I produced *Camp Candy* for the first season. For the second season, I'm a consulting producer because I've gone freelance to pursue more of a variety of projects. And of course, over this whole time I've also done lots of print jobs, merchandise art, video box art, a little bit of everything including the occasional comic book story. Coming from a print background, having learned animation, I can do a variety of different things, which appeals more to me than just having one set thing to do every day.

Q:

Did you have any official art schooling?

A:

Kind of, but I managed to avoid it to a large degree! (laughs) All through high school, I wanted to take art classes, but apparently my aptitude tests indicated that I should be taking all kinds of advanced math and physics and science classes. So I never got to take any art classes, other than drawing for the school paper. (Which was an ideal way to test out my talents.)

When I went to college, first at Cal Western University in Point Loma, and then Cal State Fullerton, I had a double major in illustration and journalism, because I felt that cartooning lies somewhere in between. But by that time, I was getting enough commercial assignments that oftentimes I would blow off my school assignments in favor of doing paying jobs. By my senior year, I dropped out of college because I felt that cartooning was

not really considered anything legitimate within the school. Yet outside of the school I was getting, if not enough work to support myself with, enough work to be tantalizingly attractive to spend more time working towards commercial goals, as opposed to academic goals.

So my real training, especially in terms of animation, came about by working in animation. Comic books certainly had prepared my draftsmanship, and from the time I was a little kid all the way up through high school, I'd sit there with a drawing pad while the cartoons were on TV. (This was before there were VCRs available, so you couldn't freeze frame anything, but I'd sit there and try to take notes and make quick sketches of character designs and layouts and things like that.)

But it wasn't until I was at Hanna Barbera and worked with old-timers and some newer guys, people like Tony Rivera and Owen Fitzgerald and Don Morgan and Floyd Norman. I mean, a lot of guys who may not be well known outside of animation, but certainly within animation who had incredible credentials, would tell me what was right and what was wrong, and I would learn by their examples. They were real gentlemen in a lot of ways and knew that my enthusiasm was genuine and so they put up with a lot from me. And essentially, I was trained on the spot there at Hanna-Barbera.

Q:

Continuing now with the work section, what does a producer do for animation?

A:

It really varies from studio to studio and project to project. As far as Saturday morning type producing, maybe the word producer is the wrong term. Actually, anybody that's a producer that's assigned to a particular show is more accurately called a line producer. This is only because we're not really that involved in either the deal making (with the network or licensee) or working with the overseas studio (setting up how much are we willing to pay for this, etc.). The line producer simply is responsible for getting film onto the air.

Usually, in Saturday morning animation, when a producer signs onto a show, the show has already been sold, or at least has started development, and whatever deal that the studio has with overseas studios has usually already been struck. The producer, for the most part, at least in my experience, is involved mainly with either assembling a crew or working with a crew that's already been hired in a department, or a number of departments. He also helps develop the characters, coming up with designs and concepts and background stylings and things hoping to meet with the approval of either the client, whether it's a network or, a toy company or whoever holds the license on a character. Many times, the writer or the story editor seems to have authority over the producer, although that certainly, in my opinion, isn't the preferable way to go.

On a day-to-day basis, the producer works with the story editor in getting stories worked out, trying to keep things on budget as well as possible, trying to keep things on schedule, getting approvals for character designs, storyboards, lay-outs, color models, background models. If animation is being done locally, to supervise that; picking music, picking sound effects; working in post-production with the editors; picking retakes; carrying the thing all the way through to final delivery.

A good producer should have a hand in just about every phase. In my case, I also usually design the main characters, do rough designs for incidental characters. I do heavy rewriting of the scripts, sometimes I write the scripts myself, do storyboard changes, and assemble a crew. Personally, I'm a very hands-on producer. When I'm producing a project, there's really not a phase that I don't meddle with in one way or another.

Q:
What do you look for in a property?
A:

Well, it's really dictated more by my own tastes than anything. I was an animation fan long before I was a professional. For me to want to become involved with a show, it has to either be very traditional or very *non*-traditional. I don't have any hard and fast rules, for example, about working on things that are based on a toy. I know some people refuse to do that sort of thing. To me, it's "is there any entertainment value inherent in it?"

My favorite characters have always been kind of hip, contemporary sort of things, like at least for its time, *The Flintstones* certainly was, *Rocky and Bullwinkle*, early Hanna-Barbera characters, *Beany and Cecil*, that sort of thing.

There's a trend towards using real life celebrities or personalities. My last two projects, Ed Grimley and John Candy shows, have been built upon that concept. I was such a fan of both

PRODUCER

of these guys' live action work, specifically from *SCTV*, that I wanted to work with them and do something that possibly would be a little bit different than your typical Saturday morning material. I don't know if those projects necessarily achieved that, but that was my initial reason for doing them.

Q:

What is your first step when you take over a project?

A:

Well, usually I want to take a look at the presentation used to sell the project. If it's something that I'm initiating myself, I'm going to meet with the person or meet with the company that has a licensed character. (If it's something of my own, obviously, being a writer and a cartoonist, I don't need to do anything but just develop some conceptual ground rules and designs and story springboards myself.)

Nowadays, certainly with Saturday morning and obviously with commercials, it's usually a pre-existing property to be developed. Presentation material is done strictly to make the sale and it may not really have anything to do with the final version of what you see on the screen. I'll get hold of that and say,"Gee, does the design work?" Does the style work? Is it even in the direction that I think it should be?

I'll do a lot of sketches and writing myself, and then hire a number of designer-artists. I'll try as many things in as many directions as possible. Usually what I'll do is I'll call artists and say "give me a day's worth of your time and let's see what your ideas are." That way I can, for say $2,000, come up with 10 radically different approaches, rather

than paying one person $2,000 to work on something for a week which may be completely outside of everybody's expectations.

Unfortunately, the way Saturday morning animation works, most producers have very little to say about story editors. In my experience, some story editors are very cooperative and other story editors consider themselves essentially above the law and outside of the production process. And that can oftentimes create enormous problems, not only in making a good cartoon, but meeting your schedule and your budget and everything else.

Once we have a Bible written, which would include the theme of the show, who the characters are, what the setting is, what the age group intended, what sort of jokes or stories or adventures are to be depicted, story springboards, the characters' relationships with one another (always an important thing), then you start developing some background ideas, styling what your environment is, doing more specific character designs.

You have to cast voices. You have to get music working that will work with the theme of the show. You get some storyboard people working. Usually, I'll try to do the board on the first episode, or at least the title of anything I work on, so I can get a style and approach set right there.

With commercials, it's vastly different because you are working under much greater pressure and the clients have much more specific ideas in mind. Usually it's based on something that's already an existing product, so you have to certainly match a certain amount of stuff to be appropriate to the product. In that case, usually the commercials that I co-

THE BEDROCK CHRONICLES

--THE EVOLUTION OF *THE FLINTSTONES*--

A VISUAL HISTORY OF **HANNA-BARBERA**'S MOST ENDURING CHARACTERS WRITTEN AND ILLUSTRATED BY **SCOTT SHAW!**

THE TEAM OF **WILLIAM HANNA** AND **JOSEPH BARBERA** HAS BEEN MAKING ANIMATED CARTOONS FOR HALF A CENTURY; THEY CREATED THE **OSCAR**-WINNING **TOM AND JERRY** SHORTS FOR **MGM**, THEN WENT ON TO OPEN THEIR OWN ANIMATION STUDIO IN 1957. THEY VIRTUALLY PIONEERED THE FIELD OF LIMITED ANIMATION ESPECIALLY FOR TELEVISION, AND SUPERVISED THE CREATION OF A LITERAL LEGION OF CARTOON STARS. BUT NONE OF THEIR VAST RANKS OF CHARACTERS CAN CLAIM ANY GREATER SUCCESS OR DURABILITY THAN THAT "MODERN STONE-AGE FAMILY," **THE FLINTSTONES.**

ACTUALLY, THE FLINTSTONES' BIRTH WAS A SOMEWHAT ROCKY ONE. BY THE LATE 1950'S, HANNA-BARBERA ALREADY HAD A STRING OF SUCCESSES WITH THEIR SYNDICATED CARTOON SHOWS, SUCH AS **RUFF AND REDDY**, **YOGI BEAR** AND THE **EMMY** AWARD-WINNING **HUCKLEBERRY HOUND**. AT THE URGING OF **SCREEN GEMS**, AS WELL AS THEIR OWN INSTINCTS FOR INNOVATION, HANNA AND BARBERA SET OUT TO CREATE THE **FIRST** ANIMATED SERIES FOR PRIME TIME T.V. →

PRRRRRRRRR

DINO

ABOVE: THE ORIGINALLY-PROPOSED CAST (INCLUDING "FRED JUNIOR") MEET THEIR CURRENT INCARNATIONS. THE 1959 VERSION WAS DRAWN BY FORMER **MGM** DESIGNER **ED BENEDICT.** **LEFT:** THE FLINTSTONE FAMILY PETS: **DINO** THE SNORKASAURUS AND **BABY PUSS**, A SABRE-TOOTHED TIGER. **RIGHT:** BENEDICT'S SECOND VERSION OF FRED (1960), SEEN BRIEFLY IN KEY SCENES OF THE SHOW'S PILOT EPISODE, "THE POOL PARTY."

produce, I also do the designing, storyboard work, help write the spot, do the lay-outs all myself. So it's a lot easier for me, because I don't have to worry about delegating any of it. I can handle it all myself, and if things aren't done right, I can only blame myself.

Q:

What do you look for when you're gathering your staff for a production?

A:

I try to hire as many people as I can that I've worked successfully with in the past. I know what to expect out of them. I've had people complain, "gee, you use all these old timers. Don't you want any young people?" And I certainly do, but it's a real relief to know that you have people that can perform. I try to avoid people who are hacks, that are just doing it by automatic response with one eye on the paycheck. But experience isn't the only thing that attracts me, but I want people that I'm not going to have to lavish a lot of time and attention (on) showing them how something's done.

On the other hand, on any given crew, I like to get at least one person in every capacity, whether it's design or storyboard or whatever, I like to try to use first timers. If nothing else, give them some of the opportunities I had when I got into the business. I try to get somebody that not only has talent, but a good attitude. Initiative is very important, too.

Nowadays, unfortunately, you meet a lot of younger people who come into the business with an attitude of, "I know it all and you can't teach me anything." Frankly, when I started, I was so de-lighted just to be working with professional cartoonists that I kept my mouth shut and my ears open and tried to learn as much as possible. I try to look for a few people with attitudes like that.

You want to find talented people. But since animation's a process that involves more than just creativity and talent, you want to find somebody that's also intelligent, understands the process, and understands what's appropriate for your audience. But above and beyond both of those is you want somebody that's reliable. You've got a deadline. You've got people to satisfy. You can have the world's most intelligent and talented person, but if they flake out on you and disappear, neither of those help.

Q:

What is the average, daily routine of a day at the office?

A:

Usually I'll try to get some work done before I even go into the studio. I try to get up early and before breakfast look over a board or read a script, or try to make some notes in a way that I can do some thinking before the phone is ringing off the hook. Now, early on in production, much of my time is spent answering the phone with people looking for work (unless it's an extremely busy season and then I'm on the phone trying to find people that will *do* the work).

Once we're in the heat of production, usually I'm meeting during the day with my designers; calling board men to make sure that the work is coming in on time, or sending work back to get revisions made; talking to the people at the network or at the agency, or with the client themselves, whoever this happens to

Shaw! designed this artwork for the cover of Get Animated! while he was still at Marvel

© *Henson Associates*

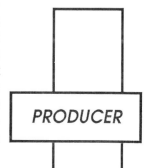

PRODUCER

be done for; checking to see if revisions on scripts are coming through in time. An awful lot of it is really almost janitorial work, as opposed to creative work.

I know a lot of people who say "ooh, a producer, that really sounds like something important." And I guess it is important, but there's certainly no glamour involved with the job. You go to recording sessions, and that's probably the most fun of any of the day-to-day jobs of a producer, but here again, none of those are ever scheduled to your convenience. It's always scheduled to the voice artist's convenience. So you could be recording on the weekend or at night. For that reason, as a producer there really is no set schedule.

You're more or less working like a fireman, where you're on call whenever you're needed. When retakes come back in and you're working with an overseas studio you want to let them know as soon as possible what needs to be redone in order to get those fixed scenes back in time to cut into your print to get it on the air. You'll go in on Saturdays, Sundays, evenings, whenever, to see the print as soon as it comes in from overseas so you can look at it on the movieola and try to get some idea of where your problem areas are. Then you have to fax the overseas studio a specific retake list, and keep your fingers crossed that you'll get most of them in time for airing.

As you go through the initial part of the season, I spend time worrying and going over the script, because everything else that comes down is based on your script, in one form or another. And not only will I work on rewriting the script, but oftentimes I'll go through the script after it's been finalized and rewrite a lot of the description involved. I'll even sometimes go so far as to break down a script into scenes and cuts, and all my screen direction, giving it to the board men, knowing that they won't do specifically what I want, but at least then they have a pretty good idea of what I want.

As you get into the season and you get your scripts more or less taken care of, then you spend more time working on getting your storyboards fixed and just your models and your backgrounds and layouts all up to snuff. The other thing that takes up much of your time the first half of production is your recording sessions, which obviously have to follow the scripts being approved.

The toughest part of production is when your scripts are finished, but you still have boards going out, and yet at the same time you have footage coming back on your earliest shows, because then you have to spend time in post-production with the editors and Telecine [transferring to video] and worrying about trying to get the footage in shape to be aired. That usually is maybe at least a month's worth of time where you're really just losing your mind, because you're actually trying to do about three full-time jobs at once. Once that's over, most of my time is spent in post-production, cutting a picture to length (I try to send them out at least 100 feet over length for editing ease), editing music, sound effects, color, etc. It's challenging because you have to do all this in a very short time with whatever footage you've received!

With most Saturday morning

animation that's animated overseas, you really spend most of your time preparing a kit. It's like preparing a kit of a model car or something, with a set of instructions, except you're preparing a cartoon kit where you're giving them all the pieces, all the designs, all the colors. You're giving them a storyboard and exposure sheets, which are essentially your instructions on how to assemble it. They do all the work and when you get it back, then you have to kind of work with them by remote control, trying to get them to fine tune it however you want it fine tuned. So I would say a producer's day is probably at least 10 to 16 hours long, and your working hours are spent more in meetings and phone calls, and you get your creative input and your real thinking input done at night and early morning.

With commercials, it's different. You're pretty much working at full speed the entire time, and there you're spending more time in meetings with the client and with the agencies, going to pre-production meetings to sell the client on what you've come up with, and then you have to have meetings with the client at literally every step of production, in terms of showing them the design, showing them the color design, showing them the layout, showing them pencil tests of animation. And you really have to hold their hand all the way through. I have to say that, on an hourly basis, working on commercials certainly *pays* more lucratively than on a series.

Q:
How much freedom do you have in production?
A:
That really depends on the production. With network shows, you really have very little freedom. The networks usually have very narrow parameters of what they want and what they expect in terms of your cartooning and the sense of humor you can show, the violence of your gags, the types of stories they want you to show, even the designs and music are under tight scrutiny.

They feel internal pressure to give a moral or give some sort of social commentary to the kids. My own feeling is a cartoon should be entertaining. My biggest battle is to keep the cartoons simple and make them funnier. I'm not against educational or moral content, but don't beat the audience over their heads with it!

Surprisingly, with commercials I find that there's slightly more freedom. Once I started doing them, I suddenly realized that the character of ad man Larry Tate in the old show *Bewitched* is much truer to life than I ever would have thought as a kid. These people flip-flop every which way possible in order to keep the client happy. Then, for the most part, the client is so busy looking at how their product is portrayed, that the rest of it is kind of up in the air, so you really have a much wider gamut of styles and ways of cutting and ways of putting across the message in commercials. That's not to say there's not a certain amount of teeth-gritting and hair-pulling involved.

Also, most cartoon commercials nowadays are animated here. You can get those nuances of acting and those little bits of business and expression that may only last for one or two frames, but can certainly make a difference in terms of how much punch or impact a certain scene has. These are "shadings" the clients respond to.

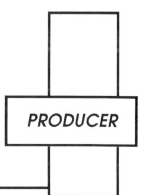

PRODUCER

I would say that the network stuff is the most restrictive, the commercial stuff has the most freedom, and somewhere in between lies the syndicated projects and feature projects.

Q:
How much freedom do you give your staff on a production?
A:

I try to give people as much freedom as I can. I mean, within any given project, you know that there are going to be certain things that are demanded. But, I feel that if people have good ideas or bad ideas, if they have ideas at all, I want to hear them. And if, for example, the model person has a story idea on how to change a storyboard to make it better, they come to me with it, I'm more than interested in hearing it. If it's valid, I'll put it in.

Everything is up for alteration, right to the point where you ship it, as long as it doesn't affect radically other phases of the show's production. Obviously, if the show's already been timed and all the characters have been designed and all the props have been designed and layouts are made, and suddenly you want to radically change a section of story, it's too late to do anything. But if you can catch it early on, my feeling is that anybody, whether they're an inker and painter, or a checker or whoever, can have an idea that's as good as its own merits! It really doesn't matter who it's coming from or what they were hired for. So I'm very open toward any contributions I can get from my staff.

Q:
What project have you worked on that you got the most pro-
fessional enjoyment or satisfaction out of, and why?
A:

Well, as I've probably mentioned already, the Flintstones are the characters that inspired me to want to be a cartoonist back when I was 9 years old. And in recent years, I've been involved with the majority of the Pebbles cereal commercials. I really feel the proudest of the Flintstones spots that I've done for Playhouse Pictures. If for no other reason than it's one of the few chances the public has of seeing new footage of those characters. It's also one of the few chances I have of having them act like they were back in the original series. Not only do I get to help conceive them and write them, but I can work with the animation locally. And the folks at Playhouse really want to do quality work, so they seem to welcome whatever input I can make at any stage of production. It is a luxury that unfortunately, for most projects I work on, I don't have.

My feeling is in a 30-second spot, if I can get a gag or two into it, with a funny reaction or a funny prop or a funny bit of business, that I've done my job. So many commercials are not entertaining, and yet they're run over and over and over again. I feel if I can make it entertaining, that's improving overall TV programming in a small way. And I would say that it's my childhood dream to work on the characters. It's certainly the most successfully animated version of them that I've ever worked on.

Q:
Conversely, what is a failed project?

A:

Well, that's an interesting question, because I'm still working on that project: *Camp Candy*. I intentionally stepped down from producer because it became so mired in network and studio politics that it was just seriously affecting my health. When things didn't work out with my successor, I was asked to get re-involved and supervise post-production on the show. I relented; I'd hate to see the show handled by unfamiliar personnel.

From the point where I came onto it, I had a definite idea of what I wanted the show to be. I think John [Candy] did as well. But as time went on, it became more and more restricted by the network's concept of what they thought it should be. And being the client, they got their wish.

The show appeals to very, very young kids. It hasn't taken full advantage of John Candy's comedic potential. Although *Camp Candy* is successful by Saturday morning standards, it just hasn't lived up to what I hoped it could have been. I'd like to produce cartoon shows that *adults* can also enjoy.

Q:

If you were starting today in the business, having gone through everything you've gone through, how would you prepare yourself to work in the animation industry?

A:

I think I probably would go to an art school that takes animation seriously and offers training in it. I've always regretted that I've never worked formally as an animator. I have done some minor-league animation, but I really don't consider myself an animator. I wish I had more experience there, only because it would give me a much better idea of what was possible, under given time and money considerations.

On the other hand, some of the schools I know locally here that specialize in animation seem to crank out a lot of talented people, but they all tend to draw alike and have very similar tastes and prejudices in what they like in cartoons. Maybe that would be both an advantage and a deficit. I really don't know.

The thing is, nowadays, to break into cartoons, you don't have the advantage that I did even a decade ago, in that there are very few really experienced people to learn from on the job. So I would say providing as much formal training as a person can for themselves, not only in watching cartoons and watching what you like, but also in acquainting yourself with the way things really are done. This book is one of the few attempts to try to give people an idea of what actually is done out there. I think that it's all too rare that anybody gets a realistic picture of what happens in animation.

Try to learn as many different phases of animation as you can; it will keep you working. That's the only way I've kept working. As things have been sent overseas and functions have been eliminated, I've become enough of a creative chameleon to keep jumping from one department to the other. The process has been not unlike climbing a rope ladder that's burning upwards from below; there's just nowhere to go but up! If you know how to function in all those other areas, it not only makes you better at whatever the job in which you are working, but gives you a fuller picture of the overall animation process.

PRODUCER

Resources

BOOKS

In 1920, the first book about animation technique was published. *Animated Cartoons: How They Are Made, Their Origin and Development* by Edwin George Lutz described techniques, tools and terminology used in animation. Supposedly, a very young Walt Disney read this book and was inspired by it. Since that time, there have been a handful of books published over the years that have tried to update that basic information.

Listed here are some current books that reportedly are still available at stores. These books will supply additional information on the process of animation. Local libraries may have other books with similar material.

In addition, the last two decades have seen a flood of animation books focusing on specific creators and studios. In particular, many books about the Disney studios, its method of operation and its characters are readily available. An inexpensive and entertaining overview of the history of animation is Leonard Maltin's *Of Mice and Magic*. A revised paperback edition (Plume 1987) is still in print.

Readers seriously interested in entering the profession of animation also should be reading books on screenplay writing, art techniques and computers. Or as Bill Scott suggested, "Read anything and everything" because it will bring more depth to your work.

A good source for ordering animation-oriented books and videotapes is *The Whole Toon Catalog*, P.O. Box 369, Issaquah, WA 98027.

Blair, Preston, *How To Draw Cartgoon Animation* #26 (Walter Foster Publications, 1990). Latest reissue of skilled animator's classic 1949 visual exploration of traditional character animation. This book is listed in almost all bibliographies of the subject. (Do *not* confuse with Foster's own book on animation, #25.)

Blair, Preston, *How To Draw Film Cartoons* #190 (Walter Foster Publications, 1990) More advanced, recent edition that is a companion to Blair's first book.

Culhane, Shamus, *Animation from Script to Screen* (St. Martin's Press, 1988). Mixed with personal opinion as well as hard facts, this comprehensive book covers the entire animation process.

Hayward, Stan, *Scriptwriting for Animation* (Focal Press, 1984). Step-by-step approach to the technicalities of animation writing.

Heath, Bob, *Animation in 12 Hard Lessons* (Heath Productions, 1972). An exercise book to help in animating scenes.

Laybourne, Kit, *The Animation Book* (Crown Publishers, 1979). Clearly written and comprehensive book filled with helpful illustrations and diagrams.

Noake, Roger, *Animation Techniques* (Chartwell Books, 1988). Lots of color stills and tightly written information on animation production, including computer animation skills.

Rubin, Susan, *Animation : The Art and the Industry* (Prentice-Hall, 1984). Basic information along with many interviews with commercial and independent animation personnel about their jobs.

Thomas, Frank and Ollie Johnston, *Disney Animation : The Illusion of Life* (Abbeville Press, 1981). Huge volume spanning over 50 years of classic character animation featuring many illustrations.

Thomas, Frank and Ollie Johnston, *Too Funny for Words* (Abbeville Press, 1987). Large book filled with numerous examples of different animation gags.

White, Tony, *The Animator's Workbook* (Watson-Guptill Publications, 1988). Provides technical information in easy-to-follow text and step-by-step illustrations.

PERIODICALS

Over the years many fine magazines have been devoted solely to animation, including Mike Barrier's *Funnyworld*, Dave Mruz's *Animania* (aka *Mindrot*) and John Cawley's *Get Animated!* publications. Some magazines such as *Millimeter, Film Comment, AFI Report, The Hollywood Reporter* and *Variety* have had special issues focusing on animation.

However, there are three animation-oriented magazines that have been publishing continuously for quite some time. These magazines offer interviews, reviews, news and articles of interest to fans as well as professionals. You may want to write and request the price for ordering an issue or the current rates for a subscription.

Animation Magazine, VSD Publications 6750 Centinela Ave., Suite 300 Los Angeles, CA 90230

Animato P.O. Box 1240 Cambridge, MA 02238

Animator Filmcraft 13 Ringway Road Part Street, St. Albans Herts AL2 2RE England

SCHOOLS

Readers seriously interested in the animation profession should first master the mechanics and fundamentals of drawing. In 1980, nearly 100 colleges and universities were offering courses in animation. For advanced work, we suggest, but do not necessarily recommend, the following schools:

California Institute of the Arts (Cal Arts) 24700 McBean Parkway Valencia, CA 91355 (Sponsored by the Disney organization, this is generally considered the best school for entering the business.)

UCLA Animation Workshop Department of Film and TV 405 Hilgard Ave. Los Angeles, CA 90024 (One of the older established animation departments at a university.)

Joe Kubert's School of Cartoon Art 37 Myrtle Ave. Dover, NJ 07801 (Although the primary emphasis is on comic art, they have had an animation division for several years now.)

Sheridan College of Applied Arts Trafalgar Road Oakville, Ontario Canada L6H 2L1 (Many of their students have gone onto professional careers in animation.)

MORE COUPON PAGE

_____Batman And Robin Serials $16.95

_____The Complete Batman And Robin Serials $19.95

_____The Green Hornet Serials $16.95

_____The Flash Gordon Serials Part 1 $16.95

_____The Flash Gordon Serials Part 2 $16.95

_____The Shadow Serials $16.95

_____Blackhawk Serials $16.95

_____Serial Adventures $14.95   ISBN#1-55698-236-4

_____Trek: The Lost Years $12.95   ISBN#1-55698-220-8

_____The Trek Encyclopedia $19.95   ISBN#1-55698-205-4

_____The Trek Crew Book $9.95   ISBN#1-55698-257-7

_____The Making Of The Next Generation $14.95   ISBN# 1-55698-219-4

_____The Complete Guide To The Next Generation $19.95

_____The Best Of Enterprise Incidents: The Magazine For Star Trek Fans $9.95

ISBN# 1-55698-231-3

_____The Gunsmoke Years $14.95   ISBN# 1-55698-221-6

_____The Wild Wild West Book $14.95   ISBN# 1-55698-162-7

_____Who Was That Masked Man $14.95   ISBN#1-55698-227-5

NAME:_____

STREET:_____

CITY:_____

STATE:_____

ZIP:_____

TOTAL:_____ SHIPPING_____

SEND TO: Couch Potato, Inc. 5715 N. Balsam Rd., Las Vegas, NV 89130